NEVER SIT
IN THE LOBBY

Oak Blue
P R E S S

www.oakbluepress.com
publisher@oakbluepress.com

ISBN: 978-1-7779391-0-6 (print)
ISBN: 978-1-7779391-1-3 (ebook)

Ordering Information:
Special discounts are available on quantity purchases by corporations, associations, and others.

For details, contact:
publisher@oakbluepress.com
www.oakbluepress.com

NEVER SIT IN THE LOBBY

57 WINNING SALES FACTORS TO GROW A BUSINESS AND BUILD A CAREER SELLING

GLENN POULOS

CONTENTS

Introduction 9

Never Fax the Facts or Ship the Shit................................**11**
    The 80/20 Rule 16

Something in Your Hand and Something in Your Mind................**21**
    Never Sit in the Lobby 22
    Never Forget a Face... 22
    WSP Factor.. 26

The Power of Three **33**
    Greed-Based Learning Factor 36

Freedom Begins with No..**43**
    $10 Million in Diamonds 45
    It's a Lead, Pick Up the Phone... 47

Always Leave a Voicemail **55**
    You Only Get Forever to Make Another Impression............. 55
    It's Better to Be Last Than Second 60

Hear Me Now, Believe Me Later......................................**65**
    Thank God It's Broken 66
    Would You Like Fries Even Though You Don't Want a Burger? 68
    Everyone's Gotta Win 72

Communication: Make Your Hello Memorable **75**

Communication: Active Listening... 77

Communication: Shit Flows Downhill, Along With Orders................ 83

Communication: Three Minutes to Paradise 86

Communication: I've Got Some Bad News............................ 89

Etiquette: Gratitude Should be a Verb...............................**93**

Etiquette: Don't Hate on Your Competition........................... 95

Etiquette: Showing Empathy.. 97

Etiquette: Get to the Point 100

Etiquette: The Mark Quigley.. 103

Sitting is Not Selling **109**

Always Ask for a Mini Tour... 112

Facts and Figures on Selling 112

Pessimism Will Affect Your Creativity 114

Rapport Building...**121**

Bottled Water Rack Factor 123

Become your Customer's Top Sales Rep 126

My Mentor Made Me Do It.. 130

Erik Vocker's Rock **135**

Bad Salespeople are Expensive (and Good Ones are Free)................ 138

Shut Up 143

The David Gleason Factor...**145**

Beware of the Customer Who Wanted a Ride in a Ferrari 152

Yes Men Get No Respect **157**

Implied Familiarity Also Breeds Contempt............................ 159

Always Check Emails 161

Checking and Leaving Voicemails—My Harshest Lesson **167**

Make Your Voicemails Count... 169

Example Script.. 172

Orders Solve a Lot of Problems 173

Cables and Connectors **177**

    Intermittent Reinforcement 178

    Ambivalent Line Loss Factor 182

    Never Get a Black Couch 184

Marconi Pizza Factor **187**

    Can't Really Motivate 'em, and the Problems with CRMs 189

    Same Difference Factor—Chabuduo 195

High Need to Add Value **199**

    No Good Deed Goes Unpunished 200

    It's Easier to Drown in the Deep End of the Pool 203

    Stolen Dreams: Multi-Port Disaster.................................. 205

    Always Ask for the Order 208

Call at Least Seven Times **211**

    Albert Martin Demo 212

    Bobby Watson Discount Strategy 215

    The Carolina 218

Dofasco Factor **221**

    You Can't Teach an Old Dog How to do New Tricks Correctly 225

    Discount to Increase Factor 227

Wittson Price Factor **237**

    Tenacious Takeaway Factor... 241

    Five by Five Breakdown Factor....................................... 242

    I Sold All the Demos... 246

    Coffee is for Closers 248

INTRODUCTION

This book of rules and advice is for the salesperson and the consumer, and was created from the knowledge I've acquired during my decades of experience in sales. While I don't have a formal writing background or consider myself to be a writer, writing and teaching are things I enjoy. Any time I can hear my own voice in my ears, it's usually a good thing for me—particularly when I'm lecturing a group on sales, consumerism, and what motivates people at a raw emotional level. To me, discussing these subjects where I know the subject matter down pat sure beats the times I engage in topics better left to others. When I do happen to stray from my comfort zone, the reaction I get are usually painful hmms and haws, umms and awws from the act of trying to BS my way through a topic. This is what I like to call "M-Sagging," or Making Shit Up Again. I can tell you from experience nothing makes a customer want to run faster than the sense that a salesperson is full of crap.

Throughout the years, I've built my belief and strategy system in the office trenches, spending thousands of hours in the field, on the phone with customers, and working with salespeople in several successful companies. My experience ranges from being a salesperson to managing teams within the companies I founded, which includes the executive level (the managers). Within my firms, I often reflect on moments and tell stories about my experiences. The traits of people or the memories of these places are used to anchor the lessons in human behavior into my memory.

This has morphed into a set of *factors*, with the names created being inspired by the person, place, or thing that first taught me the lesson. Every *factor* is a concept I've created that has a takeaway motivation for the seller and customer. By relating to these experiences, I hope that you will be able to understand the primary motivation behind the seller and the customer in order to help you adjust your negotiation strategies accordingly.

These are some of the key factors that have shaped my career. I hope these techniques can inspire, challenge, and enlighten you, too.

CHAPTER 1

NEVER FAX THE FACTS OR SHIP THE SHIT

I started selling before technology changed everything.

In 1986, we had a telegraph machine connected to a printer. When we had to send a quote, an office secretary would type it onto three-page triplicate forms of layered sheets of white, yellow, and pink carbon copies that could be separated by folding and ripping off the paper's edges. This is the tedious process we would use before we had to send the quote *in the mail*.

Within a few years, my office got a fax machine that connected to a telephone line, allowing us to receive and print data sent from other fax machines. The fax machine at the time was revolutionary, but in my opinion, was not for the better. People went from waiting a few days to a few minutes to receive their quote. This caused customers to lose their patience. Before fax machines we had about a week to put together a quote, add a letter if needed, and drop it off. Now, everything was expected *immediately*. As you might imagine, internet and email have shortened that time frame even further, from a few minutes it takes for a fax machine to process to a few seconds.

But the factor *never fax the facts or ship the shit* isn't about the underlying technology as much as it is a call to action to make sure electronic correspondence isn't the primary means of communication with your client. By this, I want to emphasize the importance of avoiding electronically submitting proposals, quotes, and literature to the customer behind a veil of false security. The same holds true for demo equipment and other items you need to provide the customer during the sales process.

For example, in my line of work, we often need to demo equipment we're trying to sell to the customer so they can verify it meets the specs or performs certain measurements. This could hold true with tools and machinery, paper products, or software. All these items should be hand delivered so you can see the whites in your customer's eyes. This face time offers you a chance to strengthen your connections with them while also completing some very important detective work. During these drop-offs, you might bump into a competitor, see their items, or notice invoices for purchases sitting on the customer's desk.

When you drop off a quote, you should always ensure that the pricing is easily visible when you pass it to the customer while guiding them to check it out. You can even say something like, "Hey Bob, let me show you, here's the unit you asked for, and you can see the total investment at the bottom." This will cause them to look and see what the bottom line is. Once they've seen the price, I ask, "So at first glance, how does our pricing look?" The goal isn't to close someone on the spot—especially if you're making high-value sales. However, if your pricing isn't within range, you'll often know quite quickly. If the customer's eyes start to bulge or open wide in amazement, these important signals will be pretty easy to notice.

Over the years, I've heard a thousand excuses from salespeople who wouldn't or *couldn't* drop off sales information and product demos to their customers. Suffice to say, fear is the most common reason, as most people don't like being rejected. When they *fax the facts*, they can *send it and forget it*. It can hurt being told no again and again, and not having to face rejection can make it easier to deal with.

Laziness is another culprit. It's simpler and more efficient to work over email. When a boss says, "Hey Jack, did you get that proposal for the new

Quantum Exasperator to Sam over at AcmeTech Solutions?" A common response might be, "Sure did, Glenn. I emailed him yesterday," confident in their mind they have done their job. At this point, I need to sit down with the salesperson and explain they're acting like a post office and not a salesperson. I could hire a virtual assistant working half way around the world for $10 per hour who can mail, fax, email, or e-quote the customer. I'm paying the salesperson to be in front of customers and "*make it to happen*," as my favorite Francophone sales guy from Quebec used to say.

Sales are won person-to-person. Over email, you won't be able to pick up clues that can give you an edge. Even if you lose the sale because of pricing or specifications, you'll gain a lifetime introduction and the ability to build a connection with the customer that could turn into a sale down the road. This also allows you to garner a deeper understanding of their thought processes, decision-making, and buying cycles.

Never fax the facts or ship the shit comes into play when the customer (who may also prefer hiding behind emails and faxes) asks for an official quote. Here's a sample conversation and scenario that often plays out with customers:

"Glenn, we're down to the final two possibilities for the agile invigorator we are looking for and you made the short list. We need an official quote showing all the options broken out with the configuration we discussed."

"No problem," I say. "When do you need this by?"

"Oh no rush, can you have it to me early next week?"

"Sure. I'll drop it off on Tuesday when I'm heading out your way (this is when I'll name a company in their area showing that we're in demand and have other buyers)."

"That's ok, you can just email it."

"No worries. I am happy to do that, but I'd like to drop a copy to you just the same," I say.

"Ok, well, I'm really busy. I don't really have time to meet with you on Tuesday. Just drop it off."

"No problem. Why don't I just drop it in the lobby?"

"Sure! If that's what you want, feel free to drop it off."

Notice how during this interaction the customer's energy changes when they realize they don't need to meet and negotiate, which can be stressful. The mindset here is that you're simply dropping off the quote in the lobby—which is true. But there's more to the process.

Fast forward to next Tuesday. Your proposal looks good and you're ready to go. You head over to the customer and on the way you pick up a dozen donuts (donuts are the sweet and sugary key to unlocking a team's soul). I suggest you do these important document drop-offs as the morning picks up, somewhere around 10 a.m. Also, the golden rule of donuts is not to bring them after 10:30 a.m., as they either won't get eaten or worse, they *will* get eaten and the customer will be mad he ate his lunch and your donuts. In general, I find donuts are best received from 8 a.m. to 10 a.m., with 10:30 being the latest.

Once you head into the lobby with your proposal documents in one hand and a dozen delicious donuts in the other, you saunter up to the receptionist and place the donuts on the counter. The air fills with sugary sweetness, and her mind starts drifting to how she can get her hands on the Boston cream, the sour cream glazed, or the apple fritter. After getting donuts out of her brain, she snaps back to reality.

"Can I help you?"

"Yes, I am here to see Bob."

"Is he expecting you?"

"Yes, he's expecting me. I'm here to drop off a quote."

At this point, 99% of the time, you're in. The receptionist calls Bob. "There's a Glenn here from XYZ company here to see you. He says you were expecting him to drop off a quote," she tells him, which is what you're doing. You're not the one asking to be invited in. "He's also got a dozen donuts for us too," she says. "Can you come down and meet him?"

Bob didn't expect to accept the drop-off personally, but given that you're providing him what he asked for and brought a dozen donuts for the office, what's the harm in making a quick trip to the lobby?

It's possible that Bob is in a meeting or busy, and that he'll simply request that you drop off the quote. At this point you could say, "I only need 30 seconds of his time to point out a few key items." And let's not forget about that Boston cream—meaning that hopefully the receptionist is falling into lockstep with your plan, suggests that Bob stop by, and reiterates that you only need a moment.

So, Bob agrees to meet you. This is the time when you can direct his attention to the pricing or any key issue you need to gauge his reaction. In some cases, Bob might invite you in and spend as much time with you as needed. However, most of the time, I would not stay beyond the few minutes required to drop off the items, get his reaction, set up a next step with him, and make a large gesture of passing over the donuts and joking that Diana at the reception desk is eyeing them up, so he'll need to be careful.

And that's it. That's the simplicity behind *never fax the facts or ship the shit*. Similarly, whenever possible you should hand-deliver any demo units and plan to set it up yourself or at least be there when the technicians are walking the customer through the process. Don't just ship the unit and leave the customer to their own devices to set it up, because often they won't even open the shipment. It'll simply sit on the dock until the day you ask for it back, and even if they do a token review of it, the mostly likely scenario is that it will have gone untouched the entire time. On the other hand, when you insist on setting it up and providing the users with a quick instructional, you get the chance to ensure everyone is comfortable with its operation while encouraging them all to spend time checking it out and realize its usefulness.

This can also be a prime opportunity to collect names of staff members so you can call them during the demo trial and see how they're liking the unit and whether it's getting use.

When you remove the demo, leave the sales material with budgetary pricing, and ask when they will be deciding to proceed.

"Oh, we'll need a couple of weeks," they say.

"Perfect, let me touch base with you a week from Friday, is that good?" you ask.

"That's great," they say. Since you now know what your plans look like for a week from Friday, you can plan your calls around your drop-in visit to follow-up in person.

The first time I explained my philosophy *don't fax the facts or ship the shit* was during a sales talk in 2005 to a group of salespeople who worked for a large manufacturer. The topic being discussed was strategies for competing in the field against the number one company. To this day, people from that talk remember me and this rule I provided. And it's been a defining factor of my career. Even to this day someone will see me at a trade show or event and say, "Hey, you're that Never Fax the Facts or Ship the Shit guy!"

The 80/20 Rule

You've probably heard of 80/20 a million times.

Common examples of this are statistics like 20% of drivers cause 80% of all traffic accidents, or 80% of social media shares are from 20% of posts, and 20% of a company's products represent 80% of sales. The one we'll discuss more in depth here is how often 80% of your business will come from 20% of your clients. Overall, this is one of the most common generalizations in business.

Keep in mind that my rendition on the 80/20 rule is a little bit different, and it requires some creative thinking to understand where you are in the pecking order. Back in the 1980s and '90s when I was selling against an 800-pound gorilla called Agilent Technologies, Inc. (a spin-off from Hewlett-Packard in 1999), the company was truly in a class of one. It was as if there were no other companies competing against them. They dominated in product segments like RF analyzers and DC power supplies, and when they landed a customer, they rarely let them go. It was very difficult to penetrate these customer relationships and displace them as a vendor. People were willing to pay the premium that Agilent commanded and of course "no one ever got fired for buying HP (or Agilent as they were then)." These 20% of the customers were delivering 80% of their business, and they focused a lot of energy on these customers for good reason.

This is where the magic starts to uncover itself a bit. When a company gets so much business from 20% of the clients, how much time, realistically, can they spend on the other customers? Other potential customers in the area buying products were never considered unless they picked up the phone and begged them to visit and sell them Agilent.

Practically, if you try to land a major customer such as Honeywell or Texas Instruments in suburban Boston, for example, that company is likely to have a master agreement with a large vendor. You could go and waste your time trying to get the scraps that didn't go to the major supplier, but what's left over? In the end, 80% of the scraps (see Broken Dreams chapter) will be diverted to their primary vendor even when there are numerous overriding benefits they should be considering.

However, the major supplier is super busy and is probably only in the area to visit Honeywell. They probably have a special vendor badge and can gain entry without checking in. They may spend their days at an assigned desk at the account with customers traipsing by all day to discuss their needs. At four p.m. when the supplier leaves to head home or back to the office to drop things off, do you think he's cold-calling NewCoTech Inc. to pursue other opportunities? This likelihood is slim to none, as he's beat from having to sell all day. What's more likely is that he simply drives back to the office with all the orders he collected at Honeywell and then heads home confident in his outstanding sales capabilities.

But don't get me wrong—it's still worthwhile to visit Honeywell to try and chip away at that 80% on occasion. You never know when the other guys are gonna mess up and an opportunity comes your way. Just realize this should not be the focus of your day. Instead, when I'm there, I visit all the other customers near Honeywell's headquarters that might have been overlooked. This allows me to turn a visit to one prospective customer (Honeywell) into a visit to seven or eight other prospective customers. I can assure you these accounts are very underserviced and happy to receive attention.

In essence, Agilent's 20 becomes my 80. I save time, money, and energy by not focusing on what I don't have. It doesn't matter what the other guys can provide. There's always someone with more than you—whether it's a better car, nicer house, or more money in their bank account.

As my mother used to say, "Don't focus on what you might lose, focus on what you get to keep."

The big company people often never expend the energy to go and find those smaller customers because they don't need to. Sometimes the smaller customer only wants to buy that big brand anyway but aren't big enough themselves to hit the bigger company's radar. So even if they end up giving them business, they won't get the same service we can offer, and this will be apparent to them since they've been ignored up to this point. In the meantime, while they've been ignored by the bigger company, I've been servicing them over and over, figuring out the company's budget cycles, long-term goals, management hierarchy, and of course the favorite donuts of the gatekeepers at the front desk.

The 20 for the other company represent my 80—and not only are those customers important to me, but they will come across as being unimportant for the other company, thereby elevating my perceived value because I'm the one who was willing to put in the extra effort. This became apparent to me when my sales area covered Winnipeg, a 500,000-population city in Manitoba, Canada.

Manitoba has a lot of government economic activity, but the weather can be brutal from mid-September into May. In fact, it gets so cold in the winter that when you park at a convenience store, you'll notice a plug in front of your car and an AC cord on the front seat. This allows you to plug in your car so the engine won't freeze while you're in the store. Obviously, it takes more than five minutes for an engine to freeze, but you get the idea. One night I left my car unplugged overnight and came out the next morning and it wouldn't turn over. I called Hertz and said, "Hey, I'm in the parking garage at the Marriot and my car won't start." They promptly asked, "Well, did you plug in the block heater last night?" Of course, I had to answer in the negative and they were like, "Ok, we'll bring you a new car and tow the one you have."

"Can't you just come and give me a boost?" I asked, which made the agent laugh.

"Not from around here, eh? We need to tow it to our indoor heated parking lot and let it warm up for a day or two, and *then* we can start it." I learned from that point on to plug in the car whenever I went indoors.

Remarkably, in the summer the beaches are spectacular, and it gets sweltering hot. To round it out, in the spring there are a million bugs, which makes the summer months the best time of year as long as you can handle the heat.

You might be thinking, *Why the focus on Winnipeg weather?* Well, salespeople have a habit of avoiding trips to Winnipeg, in large part because they can't figure out the right time to go. So, they end up making a series of excuses. "I'll go once it warms up," or "once the bugs go away," or "once it cools off a little." Instead of buying into the excuses myself, I developed a pattern of going programmatically every eight weeks, or about five to six times per year. Once while I was there I visited the Chamber of Commerce and the library and found every trade directory available. I searched from front to back looking for every company with technology in the name or for any other company that sounded like they were a tech company. Nowadays, you could just use the internet!

Every eight weeks, I would go to Winnipeg for two days. Those customers became my 20%—the 20% that the bigger companies discounted and never visited. I would typically say, "Hey, I'm coming to town. I want to show you some new products and drop off a catalog."

"You mean you literally want to come to Winnipeg?"

"I'm going to fly to Winnipeg and will come and visit you," I'd say. "I could even bring you some donuts."

These visits were always positive. And no matter what came up, if there was any inkling of an opportunity, I'd say, "Well, I'm going to be back in eight weeks. Why don't I pencil you in for a visit on my next trip?" This strategy allowed me to both secure the present and the future. If a potential customer was looking for something specific that I didn't have, I could revisit the issue and hopefully resolve it on my next visit. During each visit, I never struggled to fill up two days with calls, and even if I had down time I could always find labs and professors at the University who would share who it was that was in charge of spending money.

Over time, as I found success in Winnipeg, competitors began to wonder why they weren't killing it there, too. This is when they realized they'd never even visited because it was freezing and out of the way, and that they'd talked themselves out of going. But now, because I was finding success in Winnipeg, it was time for them to go, too. Now it was decided that there were great potential for sales in Winnipeg.

So, they booked a trip, and maybe picked up the same trade directories that I'd already studied, and would perhaps visit lots of the same people I'd already visited. Typically after striking out on their first try they would consider the trip a bust. Having not sold anything, the likeliest scenario would probably be to go back to their old routine of overlook the potential in Winnipeg once again. And while they're skipping Winnipeg, I'm planning to return again in eight weeks. This is how I turn their 20 into my 80.

CHAPTER 2

SOMETHING IN YOUR HAND
AND SOMETHING IN YOUR MIND

It doesn't matter what you sell or how much it costs.

This is one of my golden rules of selling. It doesn't matter how much or how little what you sell costs. The best part about it is it's easy to follow. If your job is one that puts you face-to-face with customers, you should always show up with *something in your hand and something in your mind.* When I make a call, I'll carry an item, be it a pen or screwdriver promo item, my notepad, and a brochure on the item I'm interested in pitching.

While this might seem like it's just about trinkets and handouts, it isn't.

In addition to having something to hand to the customer when meeting them, you need to have something in your mind to speak to them about. The topic doesn't need to be something grand like the meaning of life or the solution to cold fusion, especially if you're making a general call to drop off literature and meet new people. However, you should always have the foresight to plan your calls and research the customers prior to arriving. Make it a point to speak to them about it. In reality, when you get to the "Power of Three" chapter later in the book, you'll see it's often advantageous to have several things (but not more than three) to go over.

Think of yourself as a problem solver looking to connect your customers with opportunities, pointing out the new item in your catalog that they may like or find useful. All you need is a couple of minutes to ask them questions so they can explain what they do so you can better understand their business in relation to the products or services you sell.

That's it, at least for now.

Never Sit in the Lobby

When you do arrive to speak to a potential client, there are a few other rules you should try to abide by. Here are a few things to consider upon your arrival:

1. Arrive in the reception area.

2. Announce yourself to the correct parties.

3. While you wait, move to a position that allows you to keep an eye on the door or stairs where your client will likely arrive from.

4. Don't sit in the lobby. Stand with your attention on the present moment so you're alert and aware as they walk in.

5. Don't takes notes, play on your phone, or engage in other distractions.

6. When your client arrives, be ready to shake their hand and say hello.

Never Forget a Face

Prior to entering a business for a sales call, I always have a routine as soon as I reach the parking lot. When I started, my boss gave me a salesman's contact directory organizer which looked somewhat like the image below.

It had small cards that could be added and removed from a multi-ring binder. We called it a callbook, and could flip to a letter and see a single card for each customer.

Whenever I would reach the parking lot after meeting someone new, I would open the call book and write their name down. When I met them in the building, I always used the trick my mom taught me. When I'm introduced, I reply, "Nice to meet you, Bob," and then in my mind I say to myself, "Bob, Bob, Bob" while looking at them and burning an image of them in my brain.

When you arrive the next time, you pull out your directory. Now, in this day and age, it's probably your laptop, a smartphone, or maybe you still use a callbook. Whichever device you choose, when you pull into the parking lot of the customer, turn your car off, call up the company card, and begin to review customer names.

Look at each entry and train your brain to remember the name and the face. Usually, you will only have three or four for an account and maybe six contacts, with up to 20 contacts for your largest customers. The more names, the more important this golden rule is for getting maximum impact throughout your upcoming call with the customer.

Remember, all these rules build on top of each other. The reason you're even there is because you *never fax the facts or ship the shit.* You plan to show up in the lobby with *something in your hand and something in your mind,* and the receptionist in the lobby will ask who you're there to visit.

"John in accounting."

"Is he expecting you?"

"Yes he is, I'm here to drop off the quote he requested."

When John arrives to get his quote, your job is to turn the volume down. You ask a handful of important questions, like how does the pricing look, which companies are we competing against, and when will you make a decision? And the final golden question, "Could you take me on a mini-tour?" I usually make a statement to cut the ice even further. "I promise I won't sell anyone any insurance. And no, you don't need to introduce me to the president until the next visit." This usually gets a laugh of sorts but sets the stage that you're only looking for a quick tour of the building and you're well aware not to make a nuisance of the privilege.

So, now you're walking through the building of this big company on your mini tour. The person taking you on the tour doesn't know you from Adam, and will probably be a little trepidatious in most instances. As you walk the halls, you see a few familiar faces from the pages of your notes. Because of the golden rule *never forget a face*, you shout, "Hey Sam, how's it going? Don't forget to say hi to Steve in engineering for me." Or something like, "Hey Jack, did your wife Lucy have the baby? Yes? Oh wow, congratulations (mental note to send baby gift)."

While you're singing the song of hello to all these people, many of them will wonder, *who the hell is that guy?* Having only met you once, perhaps they're not able to place you. And then bam! They figure it out. "Oh my god, that's Glenn from SuperTech Dynamics Corp. I haven't seen that guy in two years, and he remembers me." Or they'll think, "I can't believe I didn't remember him." But trust me. These people will be impressed. The next time you visit they will be super happy to see you and will remember you for the rest of their life.

All the while, your tour guide is blown away. You've gone up one thousand percent just because you remembered a name and a face. Now they want to remember you the next time as well. He's thinking holy shit, this person knows everybody! Suddenly, you've become more and more of a known quantity. You're more trustworthy, more likable, and more liable to make a sale.

A sidebar to this story was the battle of technologies that occurred around 1985. I'd just bought a Casio handheld storage device similar to the Radio Shack TRS-80 unit below, which stored names, addresses, reminders, and was also a calculator.

I was at a sales meeting and was bragging about the revolutionary new device I had that was 10 times better than those old callbooks. I was convinced it was 10 times faster, 10 times better, with 10 times more storage. My boss Barry at the time, said, "Oh ya? Wanna bet?" As I held my trusty piece of nouveau technologie he said, "I will bet you 10 bucks my callbook is faster." He went on to say as I was getting my back up, "I bet I can call Jack at Honeywell in Cambridge way faster than you. Go!" Less than a second later, he flipped to the H tab and had the Honeywell card displayed and was reciting the phone number. I flopped and groaned and had to wait for my unit to boot up. "No fair," I said. "I have to turn mine on first."

"So did I," he said. I also ended up getting a low battery warning and never even got the account up on the display as my charger was in my briefcase upstairs in my hotel room. Your callbook can be simple or high-tech, but either way it should be dependable when you need it most.

WSP Factor

When I first told this story, it was in the late 1990s to a room full of men. I've updated the story a bit, as the original version isn't suitable today even though the underlying message is as relevant as ever.

Winning Sales Presence (WSP) refers to principles rooted in attraction, or our instinct to govern behaviors and actions intended to maximize the attraction others feel relative to the products or services we are presenting. When it comes to attraction, the heart wants what the heart wants. We have no choice in the matter. Either we are attracted to something or someone, or we are not.

Take, for instance, the Tesla Cybertruck pickup.[1] I know many people who cannot contain their excitement and attraction for that clunky vehicle, but I don't see it. Time determines whether our initial attraction level will persist, increase, or decline, and we can do things that will increase or decrease someone's attraction toward us. Someone might see a handsome, well-toned man with six-pack abs who's six feet two inches tall, and feel attracted to him. But imagine if he offers a giant smile and you notice he has cracked teeth. Or he opens his mouth and says something offensive. Your attraction level may change instantly with this new discovery.

Further, when an attraction is sparked, there's no negotiation on inherent chemistry. It's either there or it isn't. This can be hard to accept at times, but it's a basic truth if we're honest with ourselves. How many times have you heard a friend say, "They were super nice and friendly and quite good looking, but there just wasn't a spark." If it exists, time will either build attraction or in many cases it will fade over time. This is typical because actions serve to decrease attraction.

For example, chewing with your mouth open or being rude to people might immediately make you less attractive to some people. These concepts became clear to me in the '90s when I was on the road selling and visiting customers across North America. I was invited to speak and of-

---

1   "Cybertruck," Tesla, accessed September 10, 2021, https://www.tesla.com/cybertruck.

fer my insights at a sales seminar. Others were speaking on myriad topics around sales, negotiations, and presentations. My presentation came right after lunch. I stepped up to the podium and welcomed everyone back to the seminar. Then I asked them a few questions to set the stage.

"Tell me, how many people went out and left the building for a bite to eat?" I asked, and almost everyone raised their hands.

Ok, next question. "How many people went in and out of the front door of the lobby?" Again, I saw almost everyone raise their hands. "Alright, now I want to know how many people saw the jet-black Mercedes AMG parked out front two spots from the front door?" Now there was some pondering, and I would guess about 20% to 25% of them noticed this brand new car looking sweet as hell. I know I noticed it, and unlike how I feel about Tesla pickup trucks, in this case I was thinking, *Who must I kill to drive that beast home*? That baby could haul zero to 60 in under four seconds and could turn on a dime and leave you a nickel change. Five-hundred-and-fifty horsepower and every gadget available.

"Alright, let's continue. How many people noticed the three guys in the lobby just to left of the front desk dressed sharply in navy suits and looking like they work for Bodyguard Corp. You know, those guys who could either shake your hand or snap your neck without much thought, intently going over something and deep in conversation?" To this, only a few hands went up.

"And now, one final question. As we covered earlier, pretty much every one of you walked through the lobby on the way back to this meeting room. So tell me, looking past the three men and the staff at the front desk, how many of you noticed the woman with the megawatt smile effortlessly greeting people?" Without question, everyone raised their hand. "Gentlemen, so we all noticed the woman with the megawatt smile. Her personality and confidence radiated, and you took notice without her having to go out of her way to draw attention to herself.

Well my friends, that's what I call a Winning Sales Presence, or WSP for short, and when you're on a sales call, you can do what you normally do to puff up your chest and metaphorically act all macho and braggadocious, showing off your muscles with a tight fitting shirt and touting all your unbelievably fantastic virtually amazing product features and benefits. *We are the best at this and the biggest at that, no one can hold a candle to our performance, and you better act now before the deal is gone*, using the same old tactics that will garner absolutely zero attraction from the customer. Those tactics are a turn-off, and the customer is probably looking for ways to exit the meeting as gracefully as possible.

Or you can *show 'em the WSP.*

If you carry yourself with confidence and poise, and your products truly are that attractive, you don't need to *do* anything. It's more often what you *don't* do. The WSP I'm interested in showing them is my company, products, service, and the absolute pleasure it is to do business together. I'm always well-dressed, but it's my wares I'm showing in their best light.

First, stop being anti-attractive. Truthfully, stopping the mistakes is the best change you can make toward a more appealing offering. We often run into accounts all macho, showing off our product by saying look at me, look at me. You may think this is attractive, but many people will be repulsed by this attitude. The easiest way for me to explain the difference between acting macho and being a turn off with your assertiveness and *showing 'em the WSP* is to use a car analogy.

Imagine you walk in the room bragging about your new Ferrari 812 Superfast. As most of our eyes gloss over, imagine a different scenario. Instead of bragging, you walk in and someone says, "Hey Jack, didn't you just get a new car?" Rather than blather on incessantly dropping facts about the size of the engine and fancy design features, you say, "Yeah I did. You want to see it?" Jack pulls out a video on his phone with a 60-second clip highlighting the 812 Superfast in action with details overlaid and powerful theme music in the background. At just the right time the video cuts to the words "driving imagined" and ends. Perfect timing. That my friends is *showing 'em the WSP.*   that example above, you display your offering in the most attractive manner. Be subdued and transmit your natural energy.

Convey the value of your offering and allow it to shine in its proper and most attractive light. There's a rule around attraction: If someone has an attraction level to your company or product offering of 51% or higher, you can raise it. If it's 50% or lower, you have already lost the deal. So, at 50% or less you should go with the *factor I'd rather be last than second*, and save your energy for a customer who's interested. The key is to show your offering in its best light without the braggadocio.

For example, show a video of your product solving *another* customer's problem by running 10 times faster than what they're achieving now or relative to a competitor they were thinking of buying. Show customers in unscripted situations by offering bold testimonials on the results they'll achieve working with you. Make them want to experience the same feelings they're seeing existing customers express. Show the system running and allow the existing customers to provide a summary of their successes. Referrals and testimonials from validated customers are key to building attraction for your brand.

Another example is a real estate trust. They show brief clips of average investors and ask them what sort of annual growth rate (AGY percentage) they're experiencing with the North Muskoka Real Estate trust. The first person says, "I've been invested 10 years and have seen 20% average yearly growth." The next testimonial states they've also seen 20%, and so on. You're currently sitting with your money in daily savings making 0.25% per year. Does this return look attractive to you? Of course, that's the North Muskoka Real Estate trust showing you the WSP.

But sometimes, that's not enough. In this instance, you can create scenarios where the customer needs to "qualify" to work with you. Not everyone gets access to your WSP. If they did, it wouldn't be exclusive. In the example of the North Muskoka Real Estate trust, they say, "We're only focused on medium-to-high-net-worth individuals and accredited investors. You need to *qualify* and have $50,000 to invest." This turns the table and tells customers *you can't have it*, and will cause some to now work fastidiously to qualify. The more successful you can make your solutions look, the better and more confident you'll feel, and thus, the more customers will feel attracted to you. They will do the work necessary to qualify for the WSP.

A third example is something we come across in my firm often. It falls under our new vendor acquisition efforts, but in this case, they're approaching us so we call this new vendor engagement. This occurs when we get approached by a wireless technology company in another country like Spain and they say they're expanding their sales channels in Canada and would like to consider teaming with my firm. "That's great, let's set up a Zoom call and get to know the ins and outs of your product and market," we say. We get on the call and they ask us to outline our staff across Canada. We discuss our market penetration and the credentials of our salespeople. They say they'd done their homework and every customer they spoke to named my firm as the top choice, and they want to work with us. They go on to explain their technology, and we love it.

The punchline comes when we discuss commercial arrangements. They explain we can have all of Canada exclusively, but if any customers reach out to us at the factory in Spain HQ directly, they'll quote the customer. At that point, we say, "Thank you for considering us. We're ok competing with one or two other channels in our territories, but we have a firm policy not to ever compete in the territory against the manufacturer, as you control the pricing."

They may say this is their policy and seem like they won't budge on this. But we can't compete with the factory—they could easily offer customers our buy price, and we're immediately out of the competition. I bring this up as this is a common situation when dealing with companies still learning about channels and are afraid to lose business by enforcing a proper and fair channel strategy. This is again a situation where we apply the rule, *I'd rather be last than second*, and simply choose to recuse ourselves. We cut the call short, thank them for their time and say, "Look, for us this is a non-negotiable sine qua non." We hang up and don't follow up. That to us is *showing 'em the WSP* by exhibiting standards. More often than not, weeks or months later, they'll come back to us and agree to not compete against us.

When your firm is prosperous and thriving, sometimes the best thing to do is to show indirect proof. Make them see who you are and what you represent, naturally building a desire that makes them want to work with you. When you and your company are successful, you'll radiate confidence, peace, well-being, authenticity, happiness, and be pleasant and uplifting to be around. Customers will pick up on this and want to work with you.

When considering attraction, I'm reminded of a quote from Haruki Murakami's book *South of the Border, West of the Sun*: "I was always attracted not by some quantifiable, external beauty, but by something deep down, something absolute. Just as some people have a secret love for rainstorms, earthquakes, or blackouts, I liked that certain undefinable something directed my way by members of the opposite sex. For want of a better word, call it magnetism. Like it or not, it's a kind of power that snares people and reels them in."[2]

So, remember, don't go rushing in bragging about how great you are. Walk in gracefully, at the right moment, and *show 'em the WSP*. Trust me, they'll be clamoring to work with you!

---

2   Haruki Murakami, *South of the Border, West of the Sun* (New York, NY: Vintage Books, 1992).

CHAPTER 3

THE POWER OF THREE

I'm not sure what started or created the power of three, but we're inextricably bound to this concept. So much of what defines things in our world is broken up into the power of three, such as:

- Small, medium, and large
- Good, bad, and indifferent
- Snap, crackle, and pop
- Past, present, and future
- Here, there, and everywhere
- Gold, silver, and bronze

Once we wake up to this understanding, we can harness its power and make interactions with those around us more meaningful, especially during presentations. People will often drift off in meetings, captured in their own thoughts while wondering to themselves, "Hey, did I remember to feed the cats this morning? Cats, oh shoot, I was going to book tickets to that play my wife want to go to. What was that again? Something about being away, going away. Oh, right, *Come From Away*, that's it. Oh god, I better remember to do that when this is over."

You bolt back to where you are with the sound of the presenter saying, "And in conclusion…" Yikes, you might think, I didn't hear a word he said.

This is why presentations are broken down into the cardinal rule of three for public speaking:

- Tell 'em what you're gonna tell 'em.

- Tell 'em.

- Tell 'em what you told 'em.

This savvy technique will ensure that keen listeners are served all the information in a timeless method and people who tend to drift off can be snapped back to attention at the end. Even if they missed hearing it the first two times they can be saved with you telling 'em what you told 'em a third time.

While you're presenting, you should also always try to limit your topics to three. If you have four things to discuss, you need to consolidate your thoughts or split up the sessions. On the other hand, if you only have two, you need to take more time to prepare.

When you're building systems and teams, you also need to follow this golden rule of basing everything on the power of three. You only need to go back to the beginning of time to see to power of three. I mean, have you ever heard of the Holy Trinity—the Father, Son, and the Holy Ghost? Our operational structure at work is also based on the trinity of sales, operations, and finance.

In math, there are good reasons why this type of structure works. When you deviate from this structure, it causes problems in reporting and understanding how teams work together.[3] In our setup, Sales and Operations

---

3   Ira Kalb, "Marketers Must Understand The Power Of Three," Insider, May 5, 2013, https://www.businessinsider.com/using-the-power-of-three-to-your-marketing-advantage-2013-5.

departments need to understand how their teams work together, as do Sales and Finance, and Operations and Finance.

We tried adding a fourth group by splitting out Product and Vendor Management teams to make room for a larger team at the top of our organization, but look what happened when we added a fourth team:

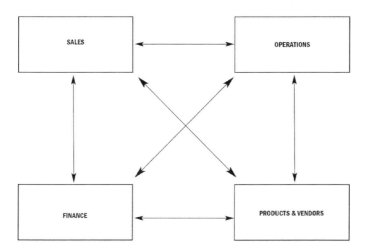

There are now three additional relationships to define and manage. This means Sales, Operations, and Finance must now integrate with Products & Vendors into their working processes. This has proved for us to be much more challenging than originally anticipated, and although we achieved the goal of including the additional staff member, it created confusion and difficulty in reporting and delegating as we continue to struggle with assigning accountability.

It took experience for me to realize the truth in the management rule of three, that any leader should have no more than three direct reports (if possible). Obviously, this isn't the case all the time, but I would argue the performance and development of more than three people is difficult, if not impossible. I would also contend that more than three people as your direct reports leads to the somebody slipping through the cracks, or everyone getting insufficient attention.

Finally, what I want to focus on with the power of three is in choices. You may think that variety is the spice of life, but too much choice leads to confusion and ultimately analysis paralysis. This can trigger a delayed purchase decision, which in some cases could trigger a whole new wave of competitors being allowed in. Choice overload occurs when "The brain, faced with an overwhelming number of similar options, struggles to make a decision."[4] Typically, when you work to limit choices you simplify the decision-making process for your customers.[5]

A classic example of this is the ubiquitous lessons learned in the Goldilocks principle. It works the same for Goldilocks deciding between too hot, too cold, too hard, too soft, and just right, but it also works in the marketplace with your customers. Why, you ask, do we need to limit ourselves with customers to this power of three rule?

First, most people can't really remember more than that. Second, when we offer too many choices, we confuse them and slow down decision making. Third, limiting to three just makes it simpler. It's hard to argue the veracity of the power of three in all things we do and used wisely three is a powerful number. Use these concepts to build strong presentations and isolate decision making with customers and employees alike.

Greed-Based Learning Factor

I love talking about the concept of *greed-based learning*, or GBL as I like to call it. It comes down to my simplistic rule of learning enough so that you can sell a product, sensing the demand a customer has for the product, and letting your own the greed kickstart your ability to learn. In essence, this means you're driven by greed to learn about a product, but you limit your scope of study to only that which is required to make the sale. When

---

4   Emily Velasco, "Scientists Uncover Why You Can't Decide What to Order for Lunch," Caltech, October 1, 2018, https://www.caltech.edu/about/news/scientists-uncover-why-you-cant-decide-what-order-lunch-83881.

5   Ira Kalb, "Marketers Must Understand The Power Of Three," Insider, May 5, 2013, https://www.businessinsider.com/using-the-power-of-three-to-your-marketing-advantage-2013-5.

properly deployed, the GBL strategy will drive comprehension and retention, and produce excitement for the product being pitched.

Salespeople and account managers have a lot of things on their plate, ranging from budget cycles all the way down to what's in stock and what's on sale. To find success you have to understand the whole gamut. While you might not have the time to be the product expert too, you do need to be knowledgeable in front of customers and handle basic questions or you'll seem weak and unprepared.

With tech products such as the ones I've sold since the 1980s, the salesman is distinctly incapable of handling half of the technical questions. For complex products, we usually have a field applications engineer (FAE) to help. But this is where the factor of GBL comes into play. In my world, we're selling high-end electronic measuring instruments that measure specialized electronic signals such as frequency, modulation, and signal to noise ratio. For complex demos, an application engineer is needed to show how to work these products.

On top of that, these products are not only super technical, but we're selling dozens of brands. If each brand has 10 products, and we have 30 vendors, that's 300 main products to know. I could spend all my spare time trying to learn the ins and outs of each product, but even then it would be nearly impossible to remember all the details of each product. Because of this, I had to come up with a triaged method of how in the world I was going to cover myself to sell these products. For me, this is where I discovered the usefulness of the GBL strategy.

The first step in my GBL process is to scan the entire range and try to establish a cursory level understanding of every product, including the product number and main measurement items. All of my product education is focused on learning what will make me money. And in reverse, by virtue of a product's profit-making potential, I'm driven to learn about it. Until then, I simply don't have the *time* to care. Now you can certainly pick hobby topics that tickle your fancy from time to time, but also realize there are limits to how many areas you can spend time learning about.

A good example of how this works would be new cars. Who has the time or inclination to learn all the features and gadgets on every new car? However, notice how when you decide to spring for a new E-Class or BMW 5 series, you have a sudden desire to learn and retain every single little gizmo, gadget, feature, and nuance your chosen car has to offer. The point is that the learning becomes effortless. It's the same with GBL. When someone wants to make a large purchase that could potentially make your week or month, you can bet your motivation (ergo greed) will kick in. This motivation will help you effortlessly learn all there is to know about the product to close the sale.

In our industry, the product managers vie for the salespeople's time so that you'll sell their products to customers instead of the other department or company's product. If, for example, you sell Xerox and Canon photocopiers, the Canon rep will want to go visit your top clients. When Xerox rep comes in three weeks later, he'll also wants to visit top customers. With 30 or 40 other product lines, how will you ever learn it all?

As a junior rep, I knew virtually nothing about the instruments and very little about these vendors. But I became the golden boy very, very quickly. None of my sales competitors in the company could figure out how I did it, as I am far from a technical genius. But based on my conversations with customers, I had a pretty good idea which customers would be best to meet with the product manager. When Sam, a product manager from the factory came to town, I would line up four or five slots for customers to meet with him. Ahead of the first meeting, we'd have a conversation.

"Just tell me about your product," I'd say. As we drive to the first call, I was often a deer in headlights. But what I was doing was listening to Sam talk about the product. While he's rattling off the list of specs, I try to pick out some of the information that will ultimately be meaningful to the customer. My mind, at this point, is still a little blurry with the facts Sam has laid on me, but that's ok.

Our first stop is to meet with Bob, an engineer with one of my key clients.

"Hi Bob, I want to introduce you to Sam from the factory," I say. "He's our product specialist on these widgets that are the greatest thing since sliced bread. Seriously, these products have the biggest bandwidth and the largest memory of any of the instruments that you can find in the industry (I'd also fire off the two specs from the drive that I remember). I'd like Sam to share a few other key points of this product."

Now it's Sam's turn. "In addition to having the best bandwidth and the largest memory of any of our products, we've also got the best resolution." When Sam finishes his presentation, the customer raises questions, and the topic turns to the customer's budget and buying cycles before we're on to the next customer.

As Sam and I continue our day together, I keep picking his brain about the product. When we meet with our next customer, I start off with the same spiel.

"Thanks for the great opening, Glenn," Sam would say. "Appreciate all those kind remarks. In addition to what Glenn said about bandwidth and memory and resolution, we also have the lightest weight among our competitors."

We go to visit the next customer, and I continue to explain how the product has the best resolution, the best memory, the best bandwidth, and the lightest weight. And because Sam says the same five things to the customer every time, I realize that's all I need to know. This is essentially GBL—pinpointing the things that matter and prioritizing them to dominate the conversation in hopes of getting the sale.

The customer might come back and say, "Is the resolution 10-bit or 12-bit?" The first time the question comes up, I'd defer to Sam because I don't know myself. But in further meetings, I'll know it's 12-bit, and I can answer that question myself as GBL memory will help me retain this information. By the time we're on the fifth call, Sam from the factory who flew hundreds of miles to do all the selling barely gets to open his mouth because I'm driving most of the conversation.

"I can't believe how well you know our products," he'd say. In the morning, I knew only the basics. But by the end of the day, I'm a bit of an expert.

During these meetings, many sales guys will just stand there, looking stupid and deferring to the product manager. Nowadays, they probably look at their phone four or five times to check whatever social media is distracting them. I learned that the number one way to politic is to be in the right place at the right time with everything. You want to know what to say, when to say it, and how to say it. The key is to *be involved*.

Remember, you're not there to hold the product manager's hand and let him do all the talking, because they measure you as a channel partner. The next day he goes out with another salesperson who ends up letting Sam answer all of the questions over and over again. Sam ends up feeling like a broken record all day and making a mental note of how much better the rep yesterday (me) was handling the presentations. My GBL showed itself in my enthusiasm for the product.

And guess what—it pays off when the product manager talks to my boss and says something like, "That guy Glenn, he's amazing. Do whatever you need to do to keep him. He's fricking awesome."

With GBL, you're taking the information directly from the person who knows the most about it and retaining enough to skim across the top, letting the AE come in underneath you and fill in all the technical details. Think about it like this. You know the five key ingredients for the recipe, but you're not trying to bake the cake.

Sometimes you have to go on a call about an instrument without the vendor with you. In those cases, you can call the regional manager or the key person and say, "What are the top five things about this product? I'm going to visit a customer and feel a little bit naked. Looking at the data sheet, what are the five things I need to point out to this guy to get his attention?" Then I basically highlight them, check them off, and commit them to memory. The next day, I walk the customer through the key points about the product.

"Hmm, you said it has the best resolution. Is it 10-bit or 12-bit?" the customer asks.

Earlier in my career, I'd have to get the answer and follow back up with the customer. The moment I got a cell phone, I could say, "Well, I don't know, but I know who the FAE is, and I can call him right now." I get Sam on the phone so he could run through the specs, and moving forward the detail would be GBL engrained on my brain.

Another aspect of GBL involves learning things that your customers will most likely be interested in. Most of your customers will only end up buying a limited fraction of your products, even if you offer 300 different instruments.

After calling the factory ahead of a visit, I'd speak to the customer and find out if the product was within their budget. Did they want something cheaper or something higher end? Are they interested in a demo?

"We'd love to see a demo," they say.

"Great." Since it's Winnipeg in February, no vendor will come with me, but it's a $20,000 instrument, and the customer wants five of them—a potential $100,000 sale.

Not wanting to screw this up, I get Sam from the factory on the phone a few days in advance of my trip to Winnipeg.

"You've gotta train me how to work this demo," I say. "Show me what to do. Walk me through the process. Teach me the functions I need to show the customer to get them interested in buying."

Because I'm greedy, I want to sell that instrument. A sales opportunity gives me the motivation to learn everything I need to know—GBL in action. Oh yeah, fear rather than greed is what reminds me to plug in the block heater on the damn car at night!

CHAPTER 4

FREEDOM BEGINS WITH NO

So often with customers, as soon as you say yes the problems start.

You come to the customer with a quote, and you've given them your best price. "You're getting really close," the customer says. "Do you think you could shave another few thousand dollars off the price?"

The losing salesperson says, "Let me go back and talk to my manager one more time. I'm not sure if we can do anything." And now the work starts all over again, and the salesperson is behind the eight ball. Now they have to come back to the customer with their tail between their legs. They've compromised their standing, and for what?

Instead, the winning salesperson will respond, "We quoted our rock bottom price. We won't be able to go any lower." This is the point when your freedom begins.

Given all the hats I've worn in the sales world, including the owner of a sales company, I've noticed a trend that salespeople think they work for their customers. They feel that they own the customer, that the customer is theirs and not the company's property. The truth is the company doesn`t own them either. We are all stewards of the relationship between the customer and the company. Unfortunately, salespeople often mistakenly put the customer's needs ahead of the company's needs. They make concessions and excuses for the customer, trying to compromise the company's standards to help the client. *Well, they need 60-day terms,* or *Why do we need a deposit from them? They're good for it!*

I always try to explain the truth to salespeople with a question. Who is your customer? They usually struggle to come up with the right answer but will blurt out the client's name who is trying to drive an even higher discount at the moment. The salesperson's true customer is the person who pays them money. That's the proper answer. Their customer is the company that signs their checks, not the client.

The ability to say no isn't just important for selling, it's a valuable life lesson, too. If you're driving a fancy car to visit relatives or friends, people might look at your set of wheels and see an opportunity.

"Can I borrow $1,000?" they ask. What do you say? You want to help everyone you can and frankly you have a thousand dollars. But you have to take care of yourself, too. This is how I respond.

"No, I can't afford it."

"Oh, ok," they say, and they move on.

The subtle point in this exchange is that by you saying you can't afford it, it causes cognitive dissonance for you because you actually have thousands in your checking account and much more in savings. You actually *can* afford it, but you can't just roll into every event and start throwing away your money to everyone who's short on rent money. To most people, *I can't afford it* is something they hear from everyone all day long every day. Do you want go to the movies tonight? No, I can't afford it. That sort of thing.

When people ask you for favors, sometimes it seems like the hardest thing to do is to say no. What is it that makes it so hard to say no? Well, primarily it's your fear of their reaction, fear of offending, fear of losing the relationship, and fear of harm.

However, saying no only requires a quick moment of pain and then you can get on with your day. Saying yes may alleviate the fear for a brief moment but opens you up to unpredictable amounts of work and commitment to deliver on what makes up the yes you're offering. You could soon be in for a world of pain while you live up to whatever you committed to. It's hard saying no, but the alternative could turn out to be much worse.

$10 Million in Diamonds

I used to work for Sears Canada in the jewelry repair department. I was lucky to get the job when my brother, who had it before me, left the position to focus on college. I had the pleasure and privilege of working for a talented watchmaker named Romeo, who had a thick Italian accent and suffered from the devastating effects of having polio as a child and struggled to walk without a cane.

Despite this, he had a specially designed car and was someone who didn't make excuses.

He loved life, and he loved women. He was always going on dates, and more often than not he would be seen out with a lady on his arm, even though due to his short stature the women were often taller than he was. In fact, he was always pushing me to ask out girls who came in for watch repairs, but we'll save those stories for another time.

My official title in the department was minor watch and jewelry repair technician, and I would fix broken chains and add new hoops and loops to broken fasteners. I could also do minor soldering repairs and buffed and cleaned jewelry for a brand-new shine. Romeo also taught me easy fixes for watches, like replacing pins in watch bands, removing links from adjustable watch straps, and buffing crystals. I enjoyed the job immensely and I tried my best to make him proud.

His lifetime goal was to open his own jewelry store, and during my time working at Sears, Romeo tendered his resignation to chase his dream. He wanted to sell fine jewelry and watches in the Niagara Region where we lived. He was so well respected that many of the workers at Sears decided to leave their jobs to work at Romeo's store.

Eventually, I moved away and started my career in sales, and the years flew by. One day, about 15 years later, I was driving along the road near his store and was amazed to see it still there. At first, I was a bit nervous, wondering if I should drop in. Would he even remember me? *What the heck,* I thought. Nothing ventured, nothing gained, so I decided to drop by.

One of the women I worked with at Sears was organizing items in the jewelry counter. She remembered me right away as she had remained close friends with my brother. She let me know Romeo was in the back and called out to him to come forward into the store. It was like a blast from the past, like no time had gone by. To me, he looked exactly the same. He still had the same thick accent, was still larger than life, and still had the same infectious, happy attitude.

We made small talk and I shared with him what had gone on in my life since the watch repair counter at Sears. It was great to see him and catch up.

"So Romeo, how's business?" I asked him.

"You know, Glenn, it's so busy. I cannot even keep up with the work. There are so many watches to fix," he said. "You know," he said in his thick Italian accent, "I could make $10 million selling those diamonds, but I'm too busy fixing those watches."

I've repeated this story more times than any other in my career. It's a reminder to make sure that your work is essential and the most profitable use of your time. For example, perhaps you should be hiring people to do paperwork or the watch repair for you. Or perhaps you need someone helping you with your laundry. Imagine saying to your kids in 20 years, "I could've made $20 million selling my widgets, but I was too busy doing laundry!"

Time is irreplaceable, and within you is a range of available deployable skills. Make the most of your most profitable skill. Don't let the watch repairs get in the way of your $10 million in diamonds.

It's a Lead, Pick Up the Phone

Whenever I say the word leads, most veteran salespeople flash back to the famous quote from the movie *Glengarry Glen Ross* where the down-on-his-luck salesman Shelley Levene, played by Jack Lemmon, demands, "These are the new leads. These are the Glengarry leads."

As a sales manager and keeper of the so-called "Glengarry leads," I've heard the question a thousand times. "Do you have any leads for us?"

It's natural to want sales leads because every sales process begins with lead generation. The sales team is tasked with taking the good leads and turning them into opportunities that they nurture and hopefully bring to a close with a successful sale. For success to occur, you'll need a constant influx of new leads and customers who are interested in buying. Though your current customers are already buying from you, that won't be enough to sustain you long-term or allow your business to grow.

Leads can be provided by the marketing team in the form of email marketing, website requests, content marketing, SEO, social media, webinars, virtual events, paid search, online advertising, or self-generated. Vendors and suppliers may also provide leads from time to time.

Many of my top sales reps develop their own leads. Instead of waiting for someone else to give them a lead, they hit the streets, either visiting accounts in their territory to garner interest in new products or by *dialing for dollars*. This is a precursor to gauging initial interest before setting up a call to drop by.

These visits give the reps a chance to put my other factors into action. When they arrive in the parking lot, they always pause to scan their company callbook or directory so they *never forget a face*. They show up in the lobby with *something in their hand and something in their mind,* such as donuts, and when the receptionist asks if he is expecting you, they boldly state with a smile, "Yes. He asked me to drop off this literature. The donuts are for everyone." As we say, every factor builds on the one before it.

Of course, not every lead is going to turn into a sale. And sometimes, you need to know when to give up on a lead. The critical thing about giving up isn't so much throwing in the towel, or a suggestion that you've lost in some way, but rather that you made the effort.

If the customer isn't interested, so be it. But when the vendor, supplier, or marketing person corners you in a sales meeting, the office hallway, or at the virtual water cooler and says, "Hey, what about that amazing lead we gave you for a flux capacitor with MajorCo just outside of Boston," you need to have a response.

"Oh yeah, I followed that one up right away," you say. "As you know, MajorCo is a key account for capacitor maker Gigantico and they have an MSA (master supply arrangement) so typically MajorCo gets all their flux capacitors from them.

"Nonetheless, I was visiting all of my key accounts around MajorCo (doing the old 20/80) and that was a perfect door opener for a drop-in visit, so I wanted to thank you for passing it on. It gave me a chance to give my contact Bob Jones a call and say, 'Hey Bob, I got a lead that MajorCo was looking for a new flux capacitor and I know you'd likely be involved in that sale. The name on the lead is for an engineer named Tom Spade, do you know him?'"

At this point, the contact can offer you angles and pieces of information to leverage. For instance, he could tell you that Tom Spade is a higher up and super important in the chain of command, or that Tom Spade is an underling and probably just kicking tires, or that perhaps he is the key guy sourcing for a new lab that will deploy the largest group of flux capacitors in the United States.

Now imagine if you just cold-called Tom Spade, and knowing he was probably being wined and dined by Gigantico since this was their key account, say, "Hey Tom, I got a good lead that named you and I wanted to know if you are a higher up, an underling, a tire kicker, or the key guy on the flux capacitor deal?" Fat chance. He may even blow you off before you get out of the gate saying, "Oh yeah, that was just for interest's sake. We're going with the new Gigantico model." You, of course, start rambling and humming and hawing, coming across as desperate and needy as you see a sale slipping through your grasp.

On the other hand, you can handle this another way. You pick up the phone and give Tom Spade a call and say, "Hey Tom, I hope you're doing well. I spoke with Bob Jones and we discussed that new flux capacitor lab you're building. By the way, congratulations on that! I'm proud to know a company like MajorCo in my home state that's building such an impressive project. Listen, I don't want to keep you on the phone, but I'm usually in MajorCo every other Thursday, and will be there this week. Typically, I'm visiting with Bob (and then start dropping two or three other names from your *never forget a face* factor) and wanted to know if I could drop off some literature on our latest products."

Don't sell them on the phone. At this point, they'll usually tell you it's fine to stop by, and that's it, you're in. You can now stack visits at MajorCo with Bob and others if possible, but worst case scenario is you go to the lobby and tell the receptionist, "Yes, he's expecting me. He asked me to drop off some literature, and sure you can have the Boston cream donut."

Once you've spent the time vetting the customer and the opportunity, you may indeed find out that the lead isn't worth pursuing, and while finishing your chat at the water cooler with the marketing rep, you can explain which of these most common reasons for non-actionable leads resulted in a dead end:

1. Despite numerous attempts to call and drop by, the customer was completely unresponsive and unavailable.

2. After talking with or visiting the customer, you determined the customer doesn't have a real need for your product or services.

3. After talking or visiting the customer, you determined the customer doesn't have the budget or financial means to support a purchase of your product or service.

4. After talking or visiting the customer, you determined the customer is hostile toward you or your company, and there's no common ground to build on to make a sale.

5. After talking or visiting the customer, you determined the customer is just a tire kicker.

The key takeaway here is to always follow up the leads you're given, be on your game, and don't offer lame excuse for why your leads are never followed up. Remember: *It's a lead, fucker. Pick up the phone.*

Salespeople can be notorious for not following up on leads and as you will learn a bit later on, it's vital to follow up on each of them. With this in mind, it's worth going over some of the reasons (or excuses) why salespeople don't follow up on leads:

1. **No lead follow-up system**: This is one of the instances when I tend to side with the salesperson. We often receive random stacks of paper, Excel lists with spotty details, vague emails, and myriad other forms, which results in inconsistent tracking, reviewing, and actioning leads. Salespeople get confused deciphering the content, and in the meantime the leads grow stale. The pile gets pushed aside and quickly forgotten, making for an embarrassing chat at the water cooler when the marketing person corners you on the status of some random lead.

Tip: If your company is going to generate leads, then it's meaningful to design a straightforward selling and follow-up process. If these leads genuinely are "the Glengarry leads," you could get a low-cost admin (even if that means recruiting on Upwork or Fiverr) to enter the leads into a system, and use ZoomInfo and other tools to find missing contact details and code the leads. Your sales team should be educated on how the leads were generated and what follow-up steps they need to take. Provide them with a sales process for all leads and train, train, train on the process. Let me be clear here. If you're the manager and the company doesn't have a clear process for lead follow up, the inaction is your fault. There should be a crystal clear, consistent message on expectations and the process for everyone to revert to as the next step.

2. **Newer, shinier leads**: This can be a real problem for most reps,

especially if they don't have a system to follow up. If they take the line of called, voice mail, left message to call back, no response, done, then you're leaving a ton of money on the table by not following up on leads. There's a good chance that a potential lead will buy something similar to the sales rep's offerings at some point. If you never get that lead into your sales funnel, you're missing out on significant opportunities.

Tip: Develop a system to call a couple of times, send a follow-up email within SPAM guidelines, which vary from country to country. In Canada, we follow CASL guidelines, where we use these rules for implied consent:[6]

- Has the recipient made a purchase or lease of goods, services, land or interest in land within the two-year period immediately before the day on which the message was sent?

- Has the recipient accepted a business, investment, or gaming opportunity offered by you within two years immediately before the day on which the message was sent?

- Has the recipient made an inquiry or application on any of the items above within the six-month period immediately before the message was sent?

- Has the recipient entered into a written contract which is still in existence or expired within two years immediately before the day on which the message was sent?

We then drop them into an automated email marketing follow-up system to drive engagement at the opportune moment. There's too much money at stake to pass over this step.

3. **I'm scared of hearing no**: This is probably the top reason salespeople don't do most things they're supposed to do. It's remark-

---

6   "From Canada's Anti-Spam Legislation (CASL) Guidance on Implied Consent," Canadian Radio-television and Telecommunications Commission, accessed September 10, 2021, https://crtc.gc.ca/eng/com500/guide.htm.

able, because anyone who's been in sales longer than a few months knows the math. Depending on your business it takes eight, 10, or maybe 20 no responses before you'll hear a yes. But ultimately you will get a yes. If that is the case, we should jump for joy every time we hear no, as we're one step closer to hearing yes. Also, no isn't a permanent answer in sales. By using other techniques in this book, like WSP, you can change someone's mind and build demand. It's your job to get through all the no responses.

4. **I don't like to seem pushy**: This whole issue of avoiding looking desperate or pushy is a huge part of what this book is about. There are many techniques to show you how to open a door or break down resistance without ever looking desperate or pushy. By adopting these techniques, you can become attractive and of value to the client, and you never need to look, feel, or act pushy.

5. **It came too easy**: People often don't value what they don't invest in. This lesson was hammered home to me when I had to pay for my college education. You can bet that when I was going into student loan debt to pay for courses, I was sure as hell invested in getting results. Also, I rarely watch football games, but once in a blue moon I'll be at a Thanksgiving dinner and bet my brother five dollars on the outcome, and I'm literally glued to the set. When my money is on the line, I'll give something my undivided attention. If you give salespeople a bunch of leads without any expectations or urgency behind them, they'll often place no value on them and under-prioritize the leads. This is where the system discussed in item one above is so important. If salespeople refuse to follow up leads and the expectations are set, then perhaps subsequent leads should start being assigned to someone else. Make them *earn* the right to get leads, and they'll be invested in ensuring they're followed up.

This ties back to *Glengarry Glen Ross* and the scene where Alec Baldwin's smarmy character Blake rants at the woeful sales team. Midway through his speech, he holds up a wooden box before pulling it away. "These are the new leads. These are the Glengarry leads," he says. "And to you, they're gold. And you don't get them. Because to give them to you is just throwing them away."[7] You want to make sure that your good leads go to salespeople who know what to with them—the salespeople who pick up the phone.

---

7   Shea Serrano, "Alec Baldwin's 'Glengarry Glen Ross' Monologue is Perfect – But Is It Accurate?" The Ringer, August 26, 2016, https://www.theringer. com/2016/8/26/16046954/fact-checking-alec-baldwins-glengarry-glen-ross-monologue-661f3662ea61.

CHAPTER 5

ALWAYS LEAVE A VOICEMAIL

While you're prospecting or making cold calls, the answer to the question: "Should I leave a voicemail?" is <u>always yes</u>.

Although many calls are not returned anymore, it will drive up your email replies when they see your name after hearing it, and connect one to the other. Many customers prefer voicemail, while others prefer face to face or want to limit communications to email. In any case, make sure you leave a voicemail for every customer in case this is one who prefers it. As earlier, your message should be no longer than 20 to 30 seconds. There's a good chance they'll pick up next time if they recognize you from your earlier voicemails. Most importantly, it's creepy to call a bunch of times and never leave a message. Trust me, they know you're doing it.

You Only Get Forever to Make Another Impression

Back in the early 1990s, I was the president of the Canadian subsidiary of a Japanese electronics company that sold precision test and measurement instruments globally. I was responsible for Canada and reported to the U.S. president who reported to a higher-up in Japan.

Every year we had a weeklong meeting to review the prior year and discuss plans for the future. It just so happened the first year in my position that the meeting was being held in Japan, and this was my first time visiting the company's headquarters and the factory in Atsugi.

Given it was at the company's home base, the normal 50-person meeting had ballooned to 100 people, with over 50 top executives from the Japan offices in attendance. Needless to say, I was nervous about making a good impression.

As it turned out, a habit I'd developed while traveling turned out to be a permanent image-setter for me. On the plane to Japan I cracked open my English/Japanese phrase book and started to learn pleasantries like "good morning" and "good afternoon" along with other simple phrases. I'd found on my previous trips abroad that learning phrases in a foreign language and using these pleasantries at a first meeting set the tone for positive engagements and memorable impressions.

So, at the meeting, when it was my turn to speak with my company's executive team watching on, I made my way up to the podium and faced the 100 people including these top 50 executives from this multi-billion-dollar company and recited a handful of Japanese phrases that I'd learned.

- *Ohayōgozaimasu.* (Good morning.)
- *Nihon de watashi o hosuto shite kurete arigatō.* (Thank you for hosting me in Japan.)
- *Kyō wa min'na genkidesu ka?* (How is everyone doing today?)
- *Nante sutekina hideshou.* (What a lovely day it is.)

After my elementary Japanese introduction, I then uttered the golden phrase that secured my place in the memories of those same 50 top Anritsu employees along with the rest of the managers from 50 other countries. I looked around at everyone with puzzled looks on their faces as I had been rambling the *only* four phrases in Japanese that I knew, and said in a curious tone, "Oh, sorry, maybe I should switch to English?"

The room exploded with laughter. I went on to give my standard eight-page PowerPoint overview following the prescribed template for Canada that contained nothing unique or of any major importance (at the time, the Canada division was only a two million subsidiary, but I ultimately grew that subsidiary to nearly $50 million, $49.6M to be exact).

Regardless of my division's size at the time, for the rest of the week and every other time I met these important executives, they would say, "Oh Glenn-san, your presentation was the best." Every single person knew my name and where I was from, and a lot of them thought I spoke fluent Japanese!

My boss, the U.S. president, was sitting beside me in the room of 100 people, and when I sat down from my presentation, he whispered to me, "You fucker. I wish I thought of doing that. Well done." Regardless, my position was established. The experience reinforced that every time you're going to encounter the higher ups, you need to act like it's the first time, because *you only get forever to make another impression.* You must assume that every time the boss—or anyone else, for that matter—comes across you in the workplace, they're taking mental notes. The goal here is to make sure you are always on your toes and looking busy.

I'm reminded of that lesson today when I walk to the back warehouse in our building. We have between four and eight guys working on the warehouse team, depending on workload and volumes. I'm always popping into the back to check on things, see how the guys are doing, and make sure everything is running smoothly. Being as predictable as I am, I usually announce myself in one of two ways. If I stumble upon the team and they're staging 30 skids that just arrived or are re-reeling cable on our cable machines, I'll usually say something like, "Throwing down, eh?" which is our slang term for you're really giving it. If, on the other hand, they just finished those chores and were taking a rest, my other quip to them is, "Oh another break, eh?" Don't get me wrong, I'm just teasing them and I'm aware of their output. However, the concept applies equally to my sales team. If I see them looking idle, I assume they're slacking off, and if I see them working the phones typing furiously or hyper-engaged with a coworker, I assume they're "throwing down."

Now imagine I see that person repeatedly in the same state. I can assume they're either lazy or a high-output worker. I always take steps to ensure I look busy. When I need a break, I leave my office and don't nap at my desk or spend hours clicking away on Facebook. By looking busy, it reminds people you actually are busy and that your time is valuable, and it subtly tells them that you're not available for idle chit-chat.

That focus also gives me freedom, further demonstrating the factor that freedom begins with no. When someone tries to push work in your lap, you can tell them (tactfully, of course), that you're busy working on a big proposal this week and swamped with team meetings the week after, establishing that you're not just sitting idly by waiting for chores and assignments.

If I'm in the kitchen making lunch, getting a beverage, or on break and someone asks me, "What's up?" I will never respond, "Not much." I always have a list of things I'm working on. You don't want to create a situation where your lack of preparedness to make another impression is left to chance.

Another aspect of this factor involves how you arrange your workspace. I don't subscribe to the empty desk approach, as this could make someone wonder if you actually work there. But I also don't respect a cluttered desk, which suggests a lack of organization. I prefer to keep my workspace free from clutter but will keep printouts and reports for the tasks at hand present in my workspace. I use a multi-monitor approach so my screens are set up in four quadrants, allowing me to stay as organized as possible with the data I need to have up on screen.

This is one way I use technology to my advantage and stay as productive as possible. On my smartphone, if I see random unimportant email messages coming in I ignore them. But if I notice an email from a coworker or customer—whether it's day, night, or weekend—I will quickly review and assess if I should respond or wait. If possible I'll also assign or move tasks to team members instantly. When I see a request from a customer at

8 p.m. on a Tuesday or 2 p.m. Saturday, I'll often answer them instantly and use the delayed send feature. I'll have the message sent in 10 minutes, 30 minutes, or an hour, for instance, so I seem on the ball but not desperate or needy.

The subject of email etiquette and inbox etiquette and techniques is up for debate. I know many people that leave huge volumes of emails in their immediate inbox and never file, tag, delete, move, or otherwise deal with them. They subscribe to the "I leave them there for posterity in case I need something" method. That's fine if you want to take that approach, but I can assure you that *you only get forever to make another impression*—and I'm going to judge you harshly. I fired an employee who had 37,000 messages in his inbox, including the email announcement of his hiring. He was famous for not replying, forgetting, or ignoring important messages but insisted his approach to handling email was adequate.

I use the zero inbox method and scan messages as they come in, determining if they're file, action or snooze for action later. This allows me to only have the next 15 minutes of emails in my face. For instance, if someone says over email or chat, "Can you approve the large order number 20002465, it's over $100K," I will immediately cycle to SAP, review the order, approve as appropriate and then reply, "Approved" immediately. Orders are the lifeblood of our business, and unless I'm in a meeting or on the phone, I see this as urgent and vitally important.

If another message pops up with someone's expense report or vacation request to approve, I'll instantly guess when I'll be finished with current tasks and snooze the message. This could be 15 minutes, an hour, later that afternoon, tonight, or tomorrow, for instance. The message will pop back at that time and I will action it. At the next appropriate moment, I'll attend to this non-urgent, important request.

Regardless, I only have present tasks visible. If I don't have an action, I tag it and hit archive so only current tasks are visible and future tasks are snoozed. Otherwise, my inbox is empty. Once again, it's fine if you want to let dozens of messages pile up in your inbox because "that's the way you do it," but rest assured I am judging you and how on top of your stuff you are. Remember, *you only get forever to make another impression.*

When I'm giving young people advice, I always tell them, "When you hear the boss's car pull up, or when you hear their door open or their footsteps coming down the hall, make sure you slide into power mode and always look engaged and busy. I find some of these tips useful for ensuring you're looking busy.

1. When the boss walks by your cubicle or office, say, "Hey, can I ask you a quick question?"

2. Make sure your work desktop is showing.

3. If possible, position your monitors so people cannot see what's displayed when walking by.

4. Engage other co-workers when you're walking about the building and engage them in work-related talk.

5. Always leave your desk looking busy but not cluttered.

It's Better to Be Last Than Second

My first job out of college was with the government. The Canadian Weather Service needed electronic technicians based at weather stations in the Arctic to fix equipment. They would put you up at remote weather stations—fly you in, drop you off for a year, and then come pick you up. I took the Arctic assignment for one year, then worked at the head office for two more years.

My boss there gave me some wise advice. "Money flows out of the end of the pen Glenn, not out of a toolbox," he said. "You're in the wrong position. You need to get into the business world. Based on what I know about you, I think you should go into sales."

Sales. Why not? I applied for a sales job and got an interview with one of the owners, a man named Kim. I was very green, and the company was looking for a seasoned salesperson. I didn't know any of that at the time, of course. For two weeks after the interview, I followed up twice a day. I called in the morning and afternoon, asking if Kim was available to talk (he was always busy).

"Did Kim make a decision on the position?" I asked the receptionist.

"No, not yet," she said.

"Ok, just tell him Glenn called." I'd call and have the same conversation, day after day after day. After 10 days, Kim finally called me back.

"We're sending you to Montreal to interview with the other owners," Kim told me. At the time while I was working for the federal government, I had this little Chevy with manual windows and no radio, the most basic functional car. I ended up flying to Montreal for this interview with the sales company. One of the owners picked me up at the airport, and he pulled up in a BMW 750.

Holy shit, I thought.

We got to the office, and there were two more 750s—all three with license plates that were one digit apart. That moment made things pretty clear for me. I was never working for the government again. This would be my new passion.

The company ended up hiring me, and soon after, Kim sat me down.

"You were the last person on my list," he told me. "You had no experience and didn't know anything about selling. I wasn't going to hire you."

"So, why did you hire me?" I asked.

"You're the only one who followed up 20 times. If you're going to follow up 20 times for the job, I know you're probably going to follow up 20 times to sell an instrument."

I worked for those guys for five years, and during that time I realized the struggle that comes with selling the third- and fourth-best brands. As a salesman, I was doing everything right. I visited all of these customers with *something in my hand and something in my mind*, flying into territories and bringing in equipment. The problem was that when you're bringing in number three or number four products, you're a long way from what people want to buy. I think of when I was a kid and my mother went to the store to buy me jeans. Levi's was the top brand and the only thing I wanted. But we couldn't afford Levi's, so my mom would end up getting me Lee jeans. They were fine and perfectly functional, even though to me they were clearly the number two brand and I didn't want to wear them.

It wasn't Levi's 80. It was the 20 that belonged to Lee. And then there were the other brands that even my mother wouldn't buy. Those other brands represented the products I was selling. No one wanted them. I'd follow up with customers until they told me no. I'd call them and they'd eventually stop answering my calls because they were either embarrassed or didn't want to hurt my feelings. The customers liked me, but the products sucked.

As bad as it is selling the third- and fourth-best brands, that territory comes with different challenges than selling from the number two spot. For number two, since the leading brand's 20 is your 80, there are still opportunities to be found and distinct advantages for many customers. You may be faster or cheaper. Think of trying to compare a Cadillac or Mercedes to a Pontiac. Some customers only need a reliable car like a Pontiac to get around.

Even if you aren't number one, you offer distinct advantages that will interest many customers. But think of it in terms of math. If the leading company's 20 is your 80, then the number two's 20 is the number three's 80, and 20 percent of 20 percent is only four percent. As the number two brand, a lot of the time you're hoping to get the 20 of the leading brand's 80. If you can quickly identify which 20 is your 20, you won't waste too much time. The problem is, sometimes salespeople go into opportunities saying, "I'm going to fight every deal until the end." Especially if you're the number two brand. You're so close to getting that business, and your brand offers solid upside. The potential customer has previously bought the top brand and is happy with their product, and they admit as much when you initially talk to them, but they're open to learning more about your offerings.

As a result, you jump through all the hoops trying to please the customer. You set up demos. You arrange to bring in engineers from the factory, which requires you to fly them in and put them up in hotels and feed them. You spend your day in meetings and strategy sessions, wining and dining. You pull out all the stops and God help you when paying the dinner bill if you brought a 'Quigley' with you. More on that later.

After all of that effort, the customer ends up sticking with the number one brand, which is what you could have predicted from the onset. So instead of going to all of the effort, you could have gone straight to the last position and won by not competing. No demo, no flying in factory reps, o wining and dining, and no sales planning and strategy sessions.

I can save my resources and my breath and my energy for the customer who's willing to take the number two brand because they recognize it has distinct advantages.

It doesn't matter how great of a salesman you are. If you're not number two and don't have competitive advantages to highlight or a value proposition, you're number three or number four, and a premium company isn't buying your products.

Selling number three or four products means you're compromising your own ability to be successful. You should always go for the number one brand. And selling past the number one or number two brand is futile.

That was the realization I reached after struggling to sell number three and four technologies, so I approached the owner. "I've got an idea to take a small slice of the technical business in wireless technology," I told him. The company was focused on electronics, but not wireless. I wanted to spin off a division focused on next-generation technology for high-frequency microwave wireless communication, or as it is known today, mmwave technology.

"Glenn," the owner told me, "Why don't you create a plan, bring it to me, and then I'll show you why it's not going to work?" Instead of going home and writing the plan, I went home and wrote my resignation, and the next day I quit and I started my first business based on wireless technologies and the new "cell phones." Just like the light bulb and the Bell telephone 100 year ago, it was doomed to be a fad, right? Only CEOs and stock brokers can justify and afford a cell phone. Isn't that funny to think about today?

Instead of worrying about third- and fourth-place brands, we went after the best of the best, and we never settled for anything less than number two. In my current company, we usually strive for number one or we just skip over it. We spend more time working with a small number of top brands instead of floundering with a whole rack of number three and four brands. When you sell the substandard brands, you need 50 of them to survive. You'll have to spread your luck across all of these different brands and once in a blue moon, you'll get an order. It's about as much fun as fixing electronic weather equipment in the Arctic.

CHAPTER 6

HEAR ME NOW, BELIEVE ME LATER

This is one of my favorite sayings, and although it may not change the course of your career in sales and management, I've crafted a reputation for how and when I use it.

Before I go further I must stop and pay homage to the *Saturday Night Live* characters Hans and Franz, played by Dana Carvey and Kevin Nealon. I remember the scene so well where they start off with, "I am Hans. And I am Franz. And we just want to pump [clap] … you up!" Later in the dialogue Franz says, "Ya. Ya, girly-man. Hear me now and believe me later—but don't think about it ever, because, if you try to think, you might cause a flabulance!"

This saying is used to precede you saying something where the idea that a truth is in front of you, but you are too preoccupied (or too "smart") to absorb it at this particular juncture. My point in saying this is, you may or may not see it from a different perspective down the road, and the importance of what I'm saying today will soon be obvious, so pay attention.

I reserve this saying when I really want my sales team to listen and take note, and they can rest assured I'm staking a lot of truth and importance in what I have to say.

For example, I might say, "Hey guys, there's new pricing coming from ACMETech adjusting the exchange fluctuations and copper prices. *Hear me now, believe me later.* This is going to affect customer purchasing decisions, and we need to start alerting them now."

Thank God It's Broken

This story will date me. It goes back to my time working at Sears, which, at one point, was called Simpsons-Sears in Canada. Now Sears is gone, which is sad because it represented something special for me when I worked there in the late 1970s.

This is also where I first started to work for my mentor Romeo, who I introduced earlier.

Sears operated on the concept that the customer was always right and had a 100 percent satisfaction guarantee. Those guarantees filtered all the way to the watch and jewelry repair shop where I worked. One time when I was working the counter, a customer came in with his bill and his beat-to-shit digital watch that he'd purchased 364 days earlier. Sears had a one-year, no-questions-asked, money-back guarantee. All the customer had to say was the magic words.

"I'm not satisfied."

"Um, you're going to have to give me a minute," I told the customer. I didn't know what to do, so I called the customer desk upstairs.

"This dude has a watch he bought 364 days ago, it's beat to rat shit, and he wants his money back," I told the customer service rep.

"Well, why is he returning it?" she asked.

"He says he's not satisfied."

"Ok, give him his money back."

"You've got to be kidding me," I told her.

"That's the guarantee," she told me. "If he's not satisfied, he has a year to bring it back. Give him his money." So, I issued the refund and gave him his money back. He took the money and walked over to the next counter and bought a new watch that was pretty much exactly the same. And I'm pretty sure what he did 364 days after that.

One day I was shopping at Eaton's, a Canadian department store on the other side of the mall, and a guy and girl were at the counter trying to return something, complaining that they weren't satisfied with the product.

"This isn't Sears. You can't have your money back," the woman at the counter told them.

This is what made Sears stand apart from others. The guarantee was unequivocal. When it came time to buy appliances and furniture for my personal apartments, naturally I went to Sears because I knew they'd be accountable if anything happened.

Whenever a product breaks for a customer, it's an opportunity to act like Sears. We now sell heavy-duty compression guns, and sometimes they break. Workers in the field rely on these tools, and when they break the workers freak out. If a customer makes a service call when his tool breaks, how are you going to help them? We're not the only company that sells these compression guns. Next time, they could buy it across the road at our competitor.

All things being equal, the customer will measure their choice on the service they've received. If we're lucky enough to have sold them a tool that broke, we have been given a gift to show the customer how good our service is so that they continue picking us—even if we're slightly more expensive.

I find that people's main reaction when a customer's product breaks is that they want to hide from the interaction, and I always tell them not to. Those circumstances provide the opportunity to build lifelong relationships. As a customer, you usually only remember bad or great service. If the salesperson isn't picking up the phone when the customer calls or doesn't return their calls promptly, it leaves a bad taste in their mouth. When this happens, they won't forget.

When the time comes to make a new purchase, the customer will be inclined to go to your competitor because you neglected them. Instead of being scared or passing the issue off to someone else, use this opportunity to show how great your service really is.

Would You Like Fries Even Though You Don't Want a Burger?

When you pull up to the drive-through window at McDonald's and place an order, you're bound to receive a question.

"Would you like fries with that?"

"Would you like to supersize your meal?"

"Would you like to add a drink?"

For them, there's always another item to sell that the customer needs. Selling the extra fries and drinks and occasionally supersizing a meal can be lucrative. Having the right sales mindset opens doors that appear closed and stops a closing door from shutting.

This reality revealed itself to me during my days selling electronic instruments, components, systems, and assemblies. These elements reflected our 80%. This was our bread and butter, and as a result we focused much of our time selling these items. But electronic instruments and other computer items aren't just stacked on a bench or strewn about in a closet. They're often stored in racks. So, we decided that in addition to selling instruments, we should also offer racks and cabinets. Essentially, for us, they became the fries and drinks. And when you think about it, every company has their fries and drinks—it's up to you to identify the up-sellable items across your product portfolio.

After we added racks and cabinets to our product portfolio, we'd get an occasional odd sale of racks from a key customer. Typically, our salespeople would sell our systems and then move on without giving much thought to selling the customer a rack. In fact, we were doing such a poor job selling the racks that the sales manager of our vendor called me. "Glenn, I'm sorry, but your sales don't warrant you buying direct any longer. We're going to let you go." This guy's whole world was racks, and he ran a factory building them. He couldn't support a partner that didn't regularly sell his items. My team wasn't earning the distributor discount, and he wanted us to act more like an end-user and buy from one of their other preferred partners.

I was embarrassed and shocked to learn that none of my salespeople were asking the customers if they wanted fries. As I came to learn, the problem ran deeper than expected. In a sense, we were doing everything we could *not* to sell racks. Our entire structure was built around not selling these lower-volume products. I pleaded with the sales manager to keep us on as a distribution partner.

"Glenn, I would need to see you at 10 times your numbers to justify keeping you on as a channel partner," he told me, and I knew that just wasn't likely. At the time, we were halfway through the calendar year.

"Look, your products are a key part of the total solutions offering, and I want to continue working with you," I said. "How about you give me six months to turn it around. If we're not clocking at the appropriate level in December, I'll quit and save you the trouble of firing us."

He agreed and I set off to learn what was going on and why we weren't selling this product that every one of our customers already bought some-place else. Since I only had six months to accomplish this task there was no time to waste.

My first step was to come up with a promotion. It happened to be the vendor's 100th anniversary, so we came up with the promo *sale100* that offered free shipping and 10% off to drive more sales. The key was to then drive momentum on the initiative. For this, I needed everyone's attention, so I sent our sales folks a note:

Guys,

Can I work with each of you specifically over the next four weeks to target 5 to 10 contacts each for racks, power bars, enclosures, grounding, etc? If we can't move enough product for our rack supplier to take notice, then it shouldn't matter if they remove us as a distributor and take away our discount level.

I will arrange support from the vendor's local support reps in each territory for sales calls as needed so we can work with buyers to establish ourselves as a

*go-to for racks, power, cables, grounding, etc. We all need to pick five to 10
key customers, and for this project we're going to LEAD with these (mundane)
products. It may drive rack sales or perhaps grounding, cables, or others.*

*If you don't need direct support that's fine too. Let's just see if we can hit our
top 80 customers. Let's call it the 80/20 plan. Eighty customers, 20 times sales
to keep our vendor.*

*Marcom will support everyone with social media postings and literature
support as needed. We'll be calling these guys after the email.*

*The final flyer is attached. We'll be sending you an HTML version today
so you can manually send emails and add to LinkedIn etc. Our bulk email
campaign will be going out midweek and then followed up by our telemarketing team.*

The idea was to change everyone's mindset on rack sales and for a brief
time, stop leading calls with our 80 and instead, lead with the 20. Many
thought my approach was insanity. To them I was turning the focus to the
fries instead of the cheeseburgers. Why waste valuable time on lower-per-
forming items? In my mind, if we didn't spend time developing our sales
of racks, we didn't deserve to sell them. This was a test and a challenge for
our sales team.

That challenge was unavoidable as we brought the promotion to the
forefront. The salespeople knew they needed eight to 10 bona fide discussions to stay onside with management. We also made thousands of touch-
points with customers through social media, and our telemarketing team
was calling hundreds of customers to drive demand as well.

I made these racks my personal mission and took it upon myself to start
or end every conversation with my sales reps by asking, "So what are they
using for racks?" When we lost a sale to a competitor, I would say, "I'm as-
suming you got them to at least buy the racks from us?" It's not a guarantee
that the competitor sold them racks, and if you can still get something out
of the sale you miss out on, *wonderful.* If they're impressed with your service, they could turn around and place larger orders with you in the future.

When the customer has no interest in our instruments, the salesperson can skip that and talk to the engineer or buyer and find out what they're using for racks. This positions ourselves as the company with the racking solution. This is the time when you can show the customer racks while also showing them your WSP (see the WSP factor for more on this) on instruments at the same time. Worst case, you'll sell them some racks. Best case, they'll realize their oversight on not evaluating your instruments and you're in on both parts of the deal.

In time, my salespeople began to anticipate my line of questioning and changed their dialogue. "Don't worry, Glenn. Yes, I sold them some racks." That's when true magic has taken over. Their normal sales process of A, B, C, win or lose might look like this, for example:

A. Prospect the customer to garner interest in our instrument, etc.

B. Do the demo and show the features and benefits, etc.

C. Close and win or lose the sale.

They now have the process of A, B, C, D or, in some cases, D, A, B, C, D:

A. Prospect the customer to garner interest in our instrument, etc.

B. Do the demo and show the features and benefits, etc.

C. Close and win or lose the sale.

D. Find out what they're doing for racks and sell them some racks.

   Or:

D. Find out what they're doing for racks and get the door open.

A. Prospect the customer to garner interest in our instrument, etc.

B. Do the demo and show the features and benefits, etc.

C. Close and win or lose the sale.

D. Having garnered interest, sell them some racks.

In short, their entire scope of attention has been broadened to include opening doors to customers to sell racks or ensuring we sell racks with every instrument. In cases where we lose the sale, we now make sure they still buy the accessories from us if at all possible. Because who doesn't love fries?

In the end, all of our effort paid off. We hit the 10 times the number for the vendor, and the following year we hit 20 times that number. Currently, we're trying some new strategies to see if we can 10 times the 20 times number, but we'll save those methods for another time.

Everyone's Gotta Win

Everyone's gotta win. It's normally classified as win-win, and is an outcome that leaves each side happy. An example of win-win is when you like pizza and your wife likes wings, so when you order the pizza and wings special from your local restaurant, she leaves you most of the pizza and you let her have most of the wings.

In the context of my business, I consider a win-win a four-way deal involving the customer, the company, the manufacturer of the product, and the salesperson. It's not just a buyer-seller arrangement.

An example of this outcome in action would involve the customer needing to hit a budget number to slide the order through without further capital requests, and you negotiate the following:

Normal Sales Price:	$100,00
Normal Cost Price:	$80,000
Requested Sales Price:	**$88,000**
Normal Sales Margin%:	20% or $20,000
Normal SP Commission %:	2.0% or $2,000

NEW DEAL

Revised Sale Price:	$88,000 (Price reduction for customer of 12%)
Revised Cost Price:	$74,000 (Reduction price for manufacturer of 16%)
New Sales Margin %:	16% or $14,000 (Reduction in margin for company of 20%)
New SP Commission:	1.6% or $1,400 (Reduction in commission for salesperson of 20%)

The customer asks you if you can bring the deal in for $88,000 or he needs to bounce it down to the head office for more funding. You approach the manufacturer and the owner of your sales company and propose the following with the intention of getting the deal right away. You'll notice hints of the Barry Watson explained later in this deal, and that's true. But in this case, you *don't* have the order.

So, when you reflect on the win-win of it all, the customer gets his request of 12% reduction in price. The manufacturer sees a reduction of 16% in the transfer price to our company. Our company reduces its margin by 20% and the salesperson also reduces his commission amount by 20%, and the deal is done.

However, I would ask the customer for other "softer" commitments like a blanket deal for the next year on all similar purchases. I would also push for them to apply for funding for extended warranties and service contracts, all at full price. When he's winning, he's more likely to concede to these highly profitable add-ons.

Below is an example of how this deal may go down in a lose-win scenario where my company stills wants the deal but the customer needs a 12% reduction and the manufacturer says no:

Bad Deal

New Sales Price:	$88,000 (Reduction in price for customer of 12%)
New Cost Price:	$80,000 (Manufacturer sees no reduction in price)
New Sales Margin %:	9% or $8,000 (Company sees a reduction in margin of 60%)
New SP Commission %:	0.0% or $0 (Reduction in commission for salesperson of 100%)

These types of situations happen all the time and they don't make sense for a sustainable business model. Wherever it's possible, look for ways to make the deal a four-way win.

CHAPTER 7

COMMUNICATION: MAKE YOUR HELLO MEMORABLE

When you walk into a room or greet a client, you want to stand out and be instantly unforgettable. Standing out at a first meeting can help you project power, be seen as a leader, and help to get the inside track on a job opening. But you also want to stand out for the right reasons. Being unforgettable isn't an innate skill, and is something you'll need to practice and perfect your techniques in order to get good at it.

Confident Body Language

This is part of why I *never sit in the lobby*. When you meet someone, you want to be standing, alert, and present a spirit of determination. Leave behind your fears, jitters, and desperation in the car after you've done your callbook factors practice. Maintain charismatic confidence and be sure to make eye contact for maximum impact.

Dress for the Part

The first thing your customer will notice as you approach is how you're dressed and how well-groomed you are. This is why it's important to always dress professionally and avoid anything provocative that may offend customers. Also remember to be mindful of branded products from vendors. If you're wearing a logo, make sure the only one you wear with customers is *yours*.

Choose clothes that are conservative and professional and make sure they're appropriate for your work environment. Finally, your shoes are among the first thing people subconsciously notice about you, so make wearing nice shoes a priority.

Be Yourself

Have friendly body language and don't seem rushed. Always use their name and show people your spirit. Limit the smiley salesperson act and be confident like you're with friends and family. People enjoy dealing with people who are authentic.

Show Recognition

If you recognize them from a previous meeting, be sure to offer an, "It's nice to see you again!" For repeat customers you've met before, you must make the effort to remember their name. It makes customers and people feel good when you greet them with their names.

Sincere Compliments

A sincere compliment goes a long way, but no doubt you've heard myriad quotes on flattery such as Dale Carnegie's, "Flattery is telling the other person precisely what he thinks about himself."[8] Or the German proverb, "Flatterers and dogs soil their own masters."[9] So, make sure the compliment is sincere and skip the flattery.

Kill the Desperation

The number one turnoff for customers is sensing a salesperson who reeks of desperation. You need to push through your fear of failure if you

---

8   Dale Carnegie, *How to Win Friends & Influence People* (New York, NY: Pocket Books, 1998).

9   Harold V. Codry, *The Multicultural Dictionary of Proverbs* (Jefferson, NC: McFarland, 2015).

want to separate yourself from the others who only dream of "making it to happen," as my old French colleague used to say. Act positive and passionate and customers will resonate with you and respond in kind. In time, as you keep practicing these skills, you'll be able to walk into any room and make a memorable and meaningful impact.

Communication: Active Listening

When you practice active listening, you're fully concentrated on what's being said. It's not just hearing someone speak. You listen with all of your senses and give your *full* attention to the person speaking.

Here are some of the ways you can practice active listening followed by an example of how I use this in daily life:

- Take on a neutral and nonjudgmental frame
- Act and practice being patient
- Don't feel the need to fill in periods of silence
- Provide the other party with both verbal and nonverbal feedback to show you are listening, such as:

  * Smiling

  * Eye contact

  * Leaning in

  * Mirroring (more on this later)

- Ask questions (see sample conversation below)
- Repeat and/or reflect back what's said
- Ask for clarification
- Summarize to let others know you understand

If you take this matter to heart and actively practice this technique, you'll not only earn trust and get a better understanding of their situations, but you'll also form a rock-solid bond with them. People love to be listened to, heard, and understood. Customers will love dealing with you if you can separate yourself from the pack of wild dogs flogging their wares and constantly looking for an opportunity to cut them off to brag about some great feature (see WSP factor). When you're practicing active listening, you have intention to comprehend while offering support and empathy to the speaker.

There are many benefits to active listening, as there are many pitfalls for not heeding this advice. The key is to find and eliminate mistakes in your techniques. I can assure you adding the habit of active listening to your behavior can have a positive impact on your life. Here a few examples:

Relationships

Active listening allows you to understand the point of view of the other person, and perhaps more importantly, to respond with empathy (see the empathy chapter). By asking questions, not talking over people, or searching for a cliché answer of advice, you show the other person that you recognize the conversation is more about them than you. This helps to validate the speaker and makes them want to talk to you longer. This is particularly important when the person is distressed. In short, this skill is invaluable and helps you avoid jumping in with a quick fix when the other person just wants to be heard.

Work

If you're a boss or supervisor, active listening at work is particularly important when you interact with your colleagues. Once you understand a problem, you can then collaborate to develop solutions. It also reflects your patience, which is key skill in the workplace. I've heard people say at least a thousand times in my job, "Oh my God, Glenn, you're the most patient person in the world." The reality is quite the contrary. Just spend a few hours with me painting or hanging shelves. But what's happening is, they're experiencing the power of active listening and getting to *feel* what it's like when someone is showing them empathy.

Social Situations

Asking questions, seeking clarification, and keenly watching other people's body language are all ways to discover more about the people you're meeting for the first time. When you practice active listening, the other person is liable to speak to you longer and will often reveal deeper truths. This is how you turn new social contacts into friends.

Here are some tips for active listening:

- Be patient, open, neutral, and withhold judgment
- Learn to recognize active listening

  * Absorb the good techniques, and reject the mistakes you see others make

- Make eye contact

  * Don't stare them down
  * Try for 60% to 70% eye contact

- Lean in and nod your head occasionally
- Folding your arms shows them you are closed off and not listening, so avoid this
- Paraphrase to let them know you understand

  * Do NOT offer advice at this point
  * Lead with comments like, "In other words, what you are saying is..."

- Don't interrupt

  * Don't plan what you're going to say
  * Focus on listening and understanding
  * Wait until the end to ensure you don't misinterpret their point of view

- Watch for nonverbal behavior, such as:

  * Facial expressions and tics

  * Tone of voice

- Shut down your internal dialogue

  * This is easier said than done, so practicing the routine below can help short circuit your internal dialogue

Show interest by asking questions at the appropriate time. Let's get to a real-world example, and then try my active listening challenge.

Example Customer Dialogue With Active Listening

You (answering the phone): Hi Bob, I hope you are doing well.

Customer: Not Really, Glenn. I'm sorry to dump this on you, but I'm really upset with you and your company.

You: Oh my. Really? Tell me about the problem.

Customer: Well, as you know, I was expecting delivery of the tester we ordered by this Friday and Lisa, your CSR, just told us the order will be delayed up to 10 days. It's Monday and I need it here by the weekend.

You: Oh wow. I can see why you're upset. Tell me how this is going to affect you.

Customer: Well, like I told you when we bought it, we're bringing a new line up the first of May (this weekend) and we need that tester installed and running to verify goods coming off the line.

You: I understand. I'm just coming up to speed on this issue as well. Tell me, did the CSR say what the delay is?

Customer: Yes, she blamed it on some bullshit COVID-19 shipping delay excuse out of Asia. Supposedly, the goods didn't get on this week's plane and won't ship for another week.

You: Yeah, we had numerous shipments bumped due to COVID-19. Seems there are certain items like PPE that take priority and can bump regular goods. I know how frustrated you must be right now.

Customer: It's more than that, Glenn. My ass is on the line. The owners from Tallahassee will be here and are set for a photo op of the new line coming up. Without that tester, I'm screwed!

You: I get it. I can see how you're pooched if this screws up.

*Custome*r: Yeah, no shit, Sherlock.

You: Ok. Well, can I ask if you're interested in creative solutions? Am I correct in understanding that the main issue is you need a tester by Friday?

Customer: I'll do anything not to look stupid.

You: Ok, I totally get it. No problem. How about this? What if we drop in a rental unit for a few weeks? I know ACME Rentals carries this unit. I can call Sam over there and get you setup. I'm pretty sure you have an account with ACME, no?

Customer: Yeah, for sure. We have like 20 things on rent from them at any time.

You: Perfect. If I set that up will that calm the situation?

Customer: Yes, for sure. Hey, thanks for listening. I know I can always count on getting you on the phone when I need to, and this is one of those times I just needed to vent. I know it's not the CSR's fault, and no one can control the delays caused by COVID-19. Thanks again, and I gotta say, you guys are number one when it comes to customer service!

You: No problem, happy to help and call me whenever. If I miss the call, I'll always call you right back.

Active Listening Challenge

I want you to try this challenge today, if possible. Your mind will probably play tricks on you when you're doing it, and your fears will want to try to force you out of frame. But if you practice, you'll see how incredible it can be.

The next time you enter a dialogue with someone, you're only allowed to say one of these *five things*. You can also use the sound "Uh-huh," and nod your head when you want them to keep going.

1. Oh, really?

2. Oh my God!

3. No way!

4. What happened next?

5. How did that make you feel?

Example

Wife: Honey, thank God you're home. I had the craziest thing happen today.

You: Oh, really?

Wife: Yes, I was walking the dog on the trails like I always do, and then she unexpectedly jumped on a lady jogging by.

You: Oh my God!

Wife: Yes, I was freaking out, and the lady was pissed!

You: No way! What happened next?

Wife: The lady stops and tears out her headphones and starts schooling me on the dog.

You: Uh-huh (nod head, raise eyes).

Wife: Yeah, she starts up with, 'Oh my God, why isn't your dog better trained?'

You: No way! What happened next?

Wife: She just keeps telling me she should report me. Of course, my blood is boiling and at this point I just want to let the dog loose on her for real this time. She was so rude and condescending.

You: Uh-huh.

Wife: And I was this close to screaming at her in my nasty voice. But then, I took a breath and thought better of it.

You: Oh, really?

Wife: I said, 'Look, I'm sorry you were so close to us. The dog got spooked and was jumping up to protect me. She's really a very good dog and I'm sorry if she startled you.' At this point, the lady backed down 70%

and kind of grumbled and said ok, no problem.

You: Really? How did that make you feel?

Wife: Well, I realized we were both just startled and freaked out, and I was able to catch myself, and as your mom always said, 'You get more flies with honey than vinegar.'

You (giggle): Oh my God. Well done, love.

Wife: Yeah, it worked out ok, I guess. Thanks for listening. How was work today?

Communication: Shit Flows Downhill, Along With Orders

When a company is buying something pricey like a forklift, even the lease payments can be expensive. You might be spending up to $100,000 for vehicles in your warehouse. When you talk with the warehouse manager, he's trying to decide whether he wants a Yamaha or Toyota.

For these major purchases, someone in senior management will have to sign off to approve the purchase. So, even though the warehouse manager is deciding which brand they should buy, it's not worth calling the warehouse manager in the beginning. A lot of salespeople might purposefully go one level above the warehouse manager's head and start there. But if it's a major purchase, you should start as high on the organizational chart as you possibly can, reaching up to and including the company president or division head, depending on the size of the company.

Sam, the company president, doesn't care about forklifts or you, but you establish rapport. If you can get any communication going with that person, establish yourself as the de facto and important supplier of forklifts for companies like his.

"I don't deal with forklifts," Sam tells me. "You've got to deal with Bob, the warehouse manager."

So, I call Bob, the warehouse manager. "I was talking to Sam, the president. We're selling a new line of forklifts. They use 20% less energy, last

20% longer, and drive 20% faster. They also carry 20% more weight. I'd like to stop by and drop off some literature. Sam the president thought it was worth giving you a call."

When you tell someone, "Hey, the president of your company thought I should call you," their ears perk up.

Bob seems intrigued and passes you along. "I know we usually use Kawasaki, but feel free to give George our warehouse supervisor a call. I know he's low on forklifts. Tell him I sent you his way."

So, now I call George and say, "George, you're the warehouse supervisor in charge of tow motors, correct?"

"Yep."

"Great. I got your name from Bob the warehouse manager. We had a great meeting. I'd been working with Sam, the president, who was kind enough to introduce me and Bob, and was blown away by our forklifts. He sent me your way. Can I come in and talk to you about them tomorrow?"

"Sure, no problem." He's now thinking, *Oh no, this guy deals with the president, and now Bob is pushing him onto me. I better take care of this.*

So, I go in and talk to George about the forklifts. "Did you know this new line uses 20% less energy, lasts 20% longer, drives 20% faster, and carries 20% more weight?"

"Wow, I didn't know that."

"Can I drop one off for a two-week trial run?"

"Sure, that sounds great."

Now flip that story around. Let's say I started with the warehouse supervisor instead, and I ask who besides him makes the decisions.

"Oh, the people upstairs. I don't know who would be the final sign-off. I just send the paperwork up."

Maybe if you're lucky, you'll get Bob the warehouse manager's name, but you're sure as hell not getting connected with Sam the president. But when you've already made those connections, when you're talking to George the warehouse supervisor, you're dropping hints every few minutes.

"When I was talking to Bob, the warehouse manager, he mentioned how the company is on a hiring spree. When I was meeting with the president a few weeks ago, he told me about longevity and the life of these things, and how important that is. I want to make sure we cover all the bases. In addition to Sam and Bob and yourself, is there anyone else we need to talk to about the forklifts in order for you to make a purchase and start enjoying the benefits of these products?"

By then, you already know the company's food chain. The president and warehouse manager are going to be signing off on the purchase, and the warehouse supervisor will oversee it. If I didn't start at the top, I wouldn't have any of that information. And climbing up from the bottom through shit is a dirty job.

That's why it's vitally important to start as high as you possibly can, even if it's to get a referral or have a two-minute call where the executive tells you, "Don't talk to me, you're wasting my time." Because even if he says that, at the very least, I can ask, "Who do I talk to?"

"Talk to George," he says, and now I've got a referral from the company president. As dismissive as it is, it's still a reference. He signed off on me talking to the next person. So you already passed that big obstacle.

And when you drop off the forklift for the two-week try and buy, you can follow up with the company president. "Thank you so much for the referrals," you say. "I dropped off trial units with the warehouse team. I know you're a busy man, but if you take five minutes and walk downstairs and check out these units, you're going to be really impressed. They're the best thing since sliced bread."

Now you've touched base with the president twice on the purchase. After the try-and-buy is complete, you can follow up with the president, manager, and supervisor to see if there's anything else they need from you in order to close the deal. You can uncover if there are financing issues or if the buying cycle is right. You've pursued the opportunity from the best angle and avoided crawling through shit.

Communication: Three Minutes to Paradise

The human attention span was measured at eight seconds, and it's worse than that of a goldfish. People are inherently impatient and quickly distracted. There's always something else they could be doing, and so many things on their mind. If you don't quickly capture someone's attention, they're thinking of things other than the words coming out of your mouth.

When you think about it, that's a lot of pressure! No wonder public speaking is one of most people's greatest fears. The elements of a great public speech haven't changed much since ancient Greece, when Aristotle wrote that the secrets to public speaking were ethos, pathos, and logos.[10]

- *Ethos* is the credibility or character of the speaker.

- *Pathos* is the emotional connection the speaker forms with the audience.

- *Logos* is the logical argument made by the speaker.

Ethos

An audience needs to see you as credible before you try and convince them of something.   Credibility is formed in layers. Does that audience respect you? Do they sense you're trustworthy and of good character? Do you emanate authority on the topic? It's fine and dandy that *you* know, but your audience must know it too.

Pathos

Pathos is an appeal made to an audience's emotions in order to evoke feeling. Your words should garner an emotional reaction—a smile, a tear, a sigh, or a laugh. Storytelling is great for establishing an emotional connection.

---

10   Jaclyn Lutzke and Mary F. Henggeler, "The Rhetorical Triangle: Understanding and Using Logos, Ethos, and Pathos," Indiana University School of Liberal Arts, November 2009, https://www.lsu.edu/hss/english/files/university_writing_files/item35402.pdf.

Logos

Logos is the logical argument you're making. Does your message make sense and is it based on facts, statistics, and evidence? If they proceed with your call to action, will the customer be rewarded with the desired outcome that you promised?

Open Strong

Your *ethos*, *pathos*, and *logos* should be on display during the opening of your presentation. You generally have three minutes to win or lose the crowd (which is a little bit longer than eight seconds, but not that much longer).

Those three minutes are crucial to forming the *hook* that encourages your audience to stay present and attentive. A powerful hook will get your audience aligned to the topic and motivated to listen. The worst thing you can do at the start of your speech is waste time on housekeeping, thank you's, or general rambling. Start strong and save the thank you's for the end.

Tell a Captivating Story

This whole book is full of stories of how I got it right and wrong in business. Storytelling is among the most powerful and consistently successful ways of grabbing attention. I find personal stories work best and show how invested you are in the topic. You can also relate a story about someone else, or tell a fable. The goal is to start strong with a 60-second narrative that launches your speech and captivates your listeners.

Rhetorical Questions

These are great for provoking thought in your audience, and since they're rhetorical, you don't expect them to answer. You want them doing it silently to themselves. Typically, you'll want the rhetorical answer they answer silently to themselves to be "yes" or "no" and to move them in the direction you want them to go.

Key Statistics

One example might be to have a rep start their presentations with the following: "According to a new study in the magazine *Worker Safety*, fork-lift injuries resulting in death are preceded 90% of the time with lapses in training. We come onsite and train workers to ensure warehouses are free of unnecessary grave injuries."

Famous or Powerful Quotes

Everyone loves a famous quote. Whenever I finish a project with a client and want to get even more involved, I love to deploy the famous Churchill quote, "Now this is not the end. It is not even the beginning of the end. But it is, perhaps, the end of the beginning."[11] Remember that the quote must always be relevant to the subject at hand and appropriate for the audience.

Power Photos/Videos

A picture is worth a thousand words. Images evoke emotion and engage attention from the audience. Adding photos can strengthen your message and make it more memorable. A good example might be showing an image of the Iron Ring bridge. In 1900, construction began on the Quebec Bridge over the St. Lawrence River. This bridge collapsed in 1907, killing 86 workers. The collapse of the bridge led to the tradition of the Iron Ring to symbolize the humility and fallibility of engineers.[12] You could then cut to a photo of your staff engineering team all standing proudly showing their iron ring on their pinkie. "When it comes to doing it right the first time, we have you covered."

---

11   "The End of the Beginning," The Churchill Society London, November 10, 1942, http://www.churchill-society-london.org.uk/EndoBegn.html.

12   Dan Levert, *On Cold Iron: A Story of Hubris and the 1907 Quebec Bridge Collapse* (Victoria, Canada: FriesenPress, 2020).

You can play video that adds the element of moving images and more importantly sound to drive emotion out of the customer audience. Videos can evoke the emotional response you need to engage customers. Avoid boring powerpoint style slideshows except to highlight your points in a dynamic presentation.

Whenever you're set to present to a customer or audience, apply the three-minute rule and use this time to convey everything of value about your pitch.

Finally, my other golden rule of public speaking is to *go last*. You can go first, which is probably second best, but never allow yourself to get stuck in the middle of forgettable presentations if you can avoid it. I'll spend whatever time is necessary lobbying coordinators at events to ensure I can *go last* and make it count. An audience always remembers the first and last presentations most.

Communication: I've Got Some Bad News

I was born in the '60s and was a teenager in the 1970s. Growing up, a lot of us did that evil thing called smoking. Even my mom smoked cigarettes, and did so in the house. That's just how it was back then.

When I was around 15 and my brother Brad was 17, my parents didn't know or chose not to know that we smoked. We were eating Christmas dinner and had relatives over. Our relatives on that side of the family all smoked. Everyone took out their cigarettes to unwind and have a long chat, puffing away at the best cigarette of the day. I looked at my brother across the dinner table and pulled out my smokes. I saw my mothers' eyes light up.

"Oh yeah, Mom, I smoke," I said. "Brad smokes too."

From that moment on, we smoked in the house just like our mom (our dad didn't smoke).

A few years later, my parents decided they wanted to get this new pull-out couch for the den in case we had extra guests. If it were me, I would have gone down to the store, picked out a couch, and brought it home.

My parents didn't do that. They spent a year, seriously, looking for the perfect couch. During that time, they must've sat on and tried out a thousand couches.

Finally, they found a couch. Hallelujah! Their patience to spend that much time hunting for something of value to them was mind-blowing to me. They brought the brand-new couch home and were overjoyed with it. Granted, it was a very nice couch and very comfortable considering it was also a pullout bed.

One day not too long after this glorious day, my brother came to me sweating like a bastard and totally freaking out.

"Oh my God, you gotta come and look," he said.

He had dozed off with a smoke in his hand and leaned against the arm rest. He'd burned a giant hole in the side of the couch. It was not some pinkie-sized cigarette burn—this hole was like eight inches across.

"Oh my God, I'm dead," he said. "They're going to kill me." He was inconsolable, and upon looking at the cavern he'd created in the side of the couch, I could see why.

I don't know how it happened, but something came to me in a flash. "Brad, just follow my lead and you can spring it on them. I guarantee you'll be ok," I told my brother. My plan was for us to bring this up after dinner.

"This is the way we're going to play it," I instructed Brad. "You're going to say this one sentence to Mom and Dad, and then I'm going to interrupt you. You're going to go, 'Mom and Dad, I have to tell you something,' and that's all you need to say. Leave the rest to me."

So, as we finished with dinner, Brad began to speak. "Mom, Dad, I've got to tell you something."

"Hang on a minute. I gotta tell you something first," I butted in, talking about my day at school, some convoluted story that meant absolutely nothing. No one cared about my story. It had no relevance. And I kept going on and on forever. As I kept talking, I could see the anxiety building in my parents' faces. They were going to snap. I kept adding onto this, spinning the story until I could tell they couldn't take it any longer. The last word hadn't even come out of my mouth, and they shifted to Brad. "What do you have to tell us?"

"Oh, I burnt a hole in the couch with a cigarette," Brad said.

"Oh my God, is that all?" they said.

"Yeah."

They were *relieved* that he only burned a hole in their new couch. Their level of anxiety waiting for him to tell them what he'd done, and their relief that it was only a burned hole, was incredible. I've never forgotten that. Was it a little underhanded? Sure. But it taught me something about human emotion and the best way to break bad news to someone.

You're not always going to be able to give your customers good news. Maybe the customer is expecting their goods to arrive by Friday, and you find out the packages aren't arriving on time. Making up a story is an option you can use too.

If you start by saying, "You know, I've got a bit of bad news for you, but I also have some good news, too," their curiosity and anxiety will be piqued, and by the time you get around to "Your delivery is slipping a week," they'll be relieved. *Is that all?* If you start off instead by saying, "Look, I've got the bad news, we're gonna be late on your product," they're going to go instantly from zero to mad. But when you take them from zero to anxious, they skip mad and will go to relieved once you deliver the news.

CHAPTER 8

ETIQUETTE: GRATITUDE SHOULD BE A VERB

When you ask people to express gratitude, most people will start with the following words: "I'm grateful for…"

I'm grateful for my wife. I'm grateful for my kids that just graduated college.

Everyone comes up with a pissing contest on a more creative thing that they're grateful for. Maybe it's grandma, the weather, or their vacation plans They think of gratitude as a noun, which it is of course. My point here is when you think of gratitude, what your grateful for, I want you to try to think of it as a verb. Thus, expressing gratitude is a verb, a word used to describe an action. Being grateful is shown by your actions. I show gratitude for my mother by visiting her once a week. I show gratitude for my key customer by donating to their favorite charity.

When I'm asked about gratitude, I usually start by saying something positive about the comments I've heard, such as, "Wow, it's amazing to hear all the special and unique things people are grateful for. I would love to dig deep and come up with something unique and compelling, but honestly, I think you guys covered it." And then, I hit them with my *gratitude factor.*

For me, I treat gratitude like it is a verb. I like to find ways to acknowledge these things and people and show them my gratitude through my actions. For instance, I'm super grateful for the quality of the local dry cleaner's work on my special sweaters and wool pants. I can't do these things at home, and I show my gratitude by throwing all my work shirts in the bag with the dry clean only and allow them to make a few extra bucks on some laundry items. I hope that by showing my gratitude by giving them more business, I can help ensure they will continue to thrive and offer me good service for a long time to come.

There are myriad ways to acknowledge and show gratitude to people in life and business. Here are just a few I practice regularly:

- **Don't complain.** Someone always has it worse than you do, and a culture of complaining will spread to those around you.

- **Give your time to people.** Be present in the moment when talking to someone. Don't be distracted by your phone, email, or all the things you have to do later.

- **Go to the person directly to express your gratitude rather than calling or emailing.** Show up in person (*with something in your hand and something in your mind*).

- **Make eye contact and be an active listener when someone is speaking to you.** You want them to understand how grateful you are. Hang onto their every word.

- **Give out compliments and be specific.** No need for confusion or to have your gratitude subverted.

- **Do the unfavorable tasks around the house or office, even when they could be assigned to others.** At the office, we don't have support staff for janitorial, so when the toilet runs over or the sink is backed up, I make sure to be readily available with the plunger in hand. I don't push this down on an underling with an "I am too good for this" attitude.

- **Be appropriately affectionate, offering a hug or warm hand-**

shake. When I see someone struggling, when appropriate, I give them a hug.

- **Offer congratulations, share praise, and acknowledge people publicly.** It feels good for people to be appreciated.

- **Share your skills and talents.** If your skills only stay with you, you've effectively wasted them. Think of all of the people who helped you along your journey. You could do the same for others.

- **Pay it forward.** Goodwill goes a long way.

- **Say you're sorry.** These are among the hardest words in the English language. Showing humility at the right moment helps others feel better and lets them know that the issue and burden isn't because of their actions.

- **Say thank you.** It's the ultimate way to verbalize your gratitude.

- **Smile often.** A smile reinforces your gratitude and lets others know how thankful you are.

The important thing to remember is not to be grateful but rather to show you are by expressing your gratitude. Many of these efforts can touch people in ways you'll never know and could resonate with them for a lifetime.

Etiquette: Don't Hate on Your Competition

Jack Ma has it right. The Alibaba Group founder is famous for his line, "Don't hate your competitors, respect your competitors."[13]

When you bash the competition, it makes you look childish, silly, dumb, and weak. It doesn't take a rocket scientist or Sigmund Freud to deduce that you want to beat your competitors. However, talking smack about them does nothing for you. It's a clear sign of weakness and leads

---

13   Fortune Magazine, "Alibaba's Jack Ma on the Companies New Frontiers | Fortune," YouTube video, December 5, 2017, https://www.youtube.com/watch?v=8G4Z93yg_o8.

customers to wonder what you're so scared about. We only put down those who threaten us.

If you're selling a top brand as you should be, then you should welcome the competition because it allows your product to be shown in its best light and provides a baseline to allow your customer to see how you're a better solution. What makes your product unique? What makes your product stand out?

Another important aspect of speaking ill of the competition is the karmic repercussions of negatively gossiping about others. As my mother always warned me when it came to gossip, "You need to stay far away from these toxic people." She made me realize early on that people who criticize others are afraid of their own shortcomings. It's also a sign of someone of feeble character and limited depth. People worth talking to have better things to discuss than gossiping about others. If you're forced to engage when someone comes up, say something positive and deflect the conversation back to the subject at hand.

Whenever the competition come up during a conversation, I always frame my response by showing how different we are. For instance, the competition may have a great product, but the product is shipped from overseas and may take 12 to 16 weeks to receive. Knowing this, you can tactfully bring up issues of delivery and when the customer discusses how quickly they'll need to receive the products.

"One of our strengths is supporting customers with fast lead times from our manufacturing plant in Tennessee. Have you looked into lead times and are they important?"

They may say, "Well yes, we need this stuff flowing to our plant in eight weeks." This allows you multiple angles of engagement. If you can meet those timelines readily, you can now say, "Eight weeks is extremely tight. With other solutions shipping from overseas, I'm sure you realize you'll be looking at over 12 weeks for delivery. If we can put the finishing touches on this deal this week, I'm confident we can hit the eight-week mark, but we'll need to get things booked with the factory ASAP. Are you ready to look over the contract and move ahead now?" This exchange allowed you to *not* bash the competition but clearly show your benefit of fast delivery and local manufacturing.

Another more concerning reason to avoid gossiping about your competitors is that you could say the wrong thing and be sued for defamation. There's a distinct risk that making false statements that damage the reputation of a person or a company can lead to a lawsuit. With the prevalence of social media and so much recorded media presence, it's possible for the defamatory statement to be broadcast through media or in print, which could open someone up to a libel lawsuit.

Again, with social media playing such a huge role in our day-to-day business image, it has also introduced what could be considered "casualness" in how we communicate. With handheld video recorders and multimedia phones popping up out of nowhere, it's super easy to get caught off guard and say the wrong thing. This can not only cause legal troubles, but it could start a Hatfield-and-McCoy situation with competitors embroiled in a juvenile back-and-forth argument.

And there's always the possibility that a competitor could one day try to poach you for your sales talent. What an awkward situation for the customer whose ear you bent talking about the competitor who doesn't match up!

In short, go with what all our moms told us when we were young: "If you don't have anything nice to say about someone, don't say anything at all."

Etiquette: Showing Empathy

Many people assume (often wrongly) that they're good at showing empathy. So let's start with the textbook definition and move on to how I like to explain applying this in the real world. Empathy is the action of understanding, being aware of, being sensitive to, and vicariously experiencing the feelings, thoughts, and experience of another."

Definitions of empathy encompass a broad range of emotional states.

Said another way, empathy is the ability to recognize, understand, and share the thoughts and feelings of someone else. This skill is fundamental and essential in demonstrating compassion in relationships. It involves experiencing another person's point of view rather than yours.

People often interchange sympathy and compassion with empathy, but there are important differences between the terms. Compassion means "'to suffer together' (…) It's defined as the feeling that arises when confronted with another's suffering and you feel motivated to relieve that suffering."[14] Sympathy is a like-mindedness between people. What affects one person similarly affects the other. It can also be an inclination to think or feel alike, display loyalty, or the capacity to share the interests of another.[15]

Some surveys indicate that empathy is on the decline in the United States and elsewhere, to the detriment of our world.[16] Displaying empathy will help you relate and connect with others so you can help them—even if sometimes that empathy comes with a selfish motive.

I find many non-empaths go straight to the cop-out, "Oh wow, I know how you feel, that sucks," and typically move on to solutions and cliché responses to bring the dialogue to a close, because in fact the situation doesn't move their objectives forward. The non-empath walks away thinking, "Wow, I'm such a good friend or associate, listening to all those problems and solving them too." The other person, more often than not, is left with the hollow feeling that the other person is an insensitive jerk. A non-empath will likely be egotistical and prioritize themselves over others most or all of the time.

When you see someone experiencing something that requires empathy, try to practice active and purposeful listening. Before responding to any-

---

14 "What Is Compassion?" Greater Good Magazine, accessed September 13, 2021, https://greatergood.berkeley.edu/topic/compassion/definition.

15 "sympathy," Merriam-Webster, accessed September 13, 2021, https://www.merriam-webster.com/dictionary/sympathy.

16 "Speaking of Psychology: The decline of empathy and the rise of narcissism," American Psychology Association (APA), December 2019, https://www.apa.org/research/action/speaking-of-psychology/empathy-narcissism.

thing, true empathy requires you to short circuit your own mind's thinking and climb inside the other person's world in order to process what they're going through. You have to *be* them, and then set your mind to think about how the situation makes you feel. While it might be difficult, you need to feel what they feel, not know how they feel. Here are a few ways to show empathy to others:

- *Listen.* Practice the active listening techniques outlined elsewhere in this book, and if you want to show empathy, you need to genuinely listen. This means you'll need to put down your phone and stop thinking of your weekend plans.

- *Share.* Just listening won't build a connection. Open up and share personal things about yourself if you want to deepen the relationship with another person.

- *Appropriate physical affection.* Depending on social distancing guidelines and your familiarity with the person (if you're unsure, ask first if it's ok), give them a hug or even a heartfelt handshake. You'll both feel amazing.

- *Don't judge.* This is super hard, but you need to avoid judging others.

- *Avoid prejudice.* If you're indeed in another person's shoes, you shouldn't be applying your prejudices. For instance, judging someone because they're "from the wrong side of the tracks," or "born with a silver spoon" will keep you from getting to know the individual on a deeper level.

- *Offer appropriate help.* If you genuinely feel what someone is going through, you'll want to make life easier for them. At the core of empathy is genuinely wanting to offer your help.

- *Make others feel important.* Do you remember what mother used to say? "Treat others as you wish to be treated." Show them they're important and realize you aren't superior to anyone else.

The rewards to you will receive from this act of kindness are:

- *Better health:* Empathy makes you compassionate and better equipped to handle stress.
- *Improved communication skills:* Listening and learning about others will strengthen your communication skills and help to understand them more easily.
- *Work benefits:* Practicing give and take in work negotiations will help drive a win-win scenario. This also helps to build teamwork so that everyone is more likely to work as a unit instead of individuals.
- *Social/affiliative behavior.* When people look out for one another, we build a better society.

Empathy keeps you grounded, and it can help in your career, too, allowing you to view the world through others' eyes. Stepping into customers' shoes aligns you with their needs. In the process, maybe you can help them solve some of their problems and make life a little easier.

Etiquette: Get to the Point

I receive a lot of phone calls every week, and I coach people every day who make just as many. As I went over in previous chapters, I always answer the phone when possible. Therefore, if a salesperson makes the effort of getting my contact details, they're likely to catch me directly without any barriers. They can speak directly with the cofounder, vice president, and general manager who very often makes the final decision.

Given the large number of calls I get, I've developed a massive pet peeve. Let me run you through a typical conversation.

"Glenn Poulos, good afternoon."

"Oh hi, Glenn, I'm so glad I caught you." Already, three to four seconds of my short patience have expired. "How are you?" One to two seconds more of my short patience expired.

"I'm fine thanks. And you?" I always say this to not be rude.

"Oh wow, I'm doing really well, Glenn, thank you for asking." Three to four seconds more of my short patience has expired, and at this point I'm already at the point where I don't want to talk any longer. And then they drop the killer line that totally throws off my calm

"So, Glenn, did I catch you at a good time?" Five to six seconds more of my short patience has expired. What kind of question is that? If it wasn't an acceptable time, I wouldn't have picked up the phone, right?

"Umm, well, yes, it's fine." I'm suffering from cognitive dissonance over this because my words are completely out of line with my feelings. We're now at 20 to 30 seconds of wasted time and I don't even know who the fuck they are!

"Ok great. Listen I'm Bob Moore from ACME Insurance and we're currently saving companies like yours 20% to 30% on premiums with our new flex-rate program. Would you be interested in setting up a zoom call for a presentation?"

"Well Bob, the director of finance handles all the insurance needs. Let me transfer you. Her name is Judy."

I hang up frustrated every time over these exchanges. Nonetheless, I'm running a business and I don't believe in rejecting them with the line, "We're happy with our insurance and I don't want you to save us any money." I'll pass him on, but remember the important *factor you only get forever to make another impression*, and Bob has failed.

So, alternatively, this is how Bob could have handled the call.

"Glenn Poulos, good afternoon."

"Oh hi, Glenn, I hope you're doing well (that phrase is uncommon and does not solicit the automatic and you).

"I am, thanks."

"That's good to hear. I'm Bob Moore from ACME Insurance. I'm calling because we're currently saving companies like yours 20% to 30% on premiums with our new flex-rate program. Would you be interested in setting up a zoom call for a presentation?"

"Well Bob, the director of finance handles all the insurance needs. I just sign off as final authority. Let me transfer you. Her name is Judy and here's a hint for you. She loves dogs." Notice how I'm giving him pointers for *not* wasting my time with useless pleasantries. As a reward for his efficient approach, he gained information that I was the final signoff and that Judy loves dogs—invaluable information for him to use later in the cycle.

Obviously, there are times where a little more or a little less is required on a call but the key is being as brief as possible and avoiding all the helper phrases that gum up a conversation. Here are some basic rules to follow when you're trying to make the most of every phone call.

- *Greet them warmly*: "Hi Glenn, I hope you're doing well?" acknowledges the recipient's name. We love hearing our name and respond to it. It also helps show familiarity and respect.

- *Personalize the message to their company*: "We had success showing companies like yours an easy way to reduce waste charges by 30% to 40%." This shows you're calling with something of value and aren't trying to sell them something right away.

- *Use callbook factors*: Drop the name of a coworker. "Sally in finance told me to call you." This can help get your foot in the door more easily.

- *Reference LinkedIn details*: "I saw on your LinkedIn you are expanding overseas. I'm certain our freight management solution can streamline shipments and save on customs charges."

- *Bring up pain points*: Reference companies they can relate to, perhaps even a competitor, and note how they experience some of the same issues. "We've been handling 3D printing for BNB Enterprises and they were experiencing problems with throughput. I wondered if you had similar issues." This will get them wondering and wanting to hear the rest of the story. If it's a competitor they'll be interested in what they can learn during the sales process about what the competitor is doing (naturally you won't reveal details of other customers like that).

- *Appropriate small talk*: The best way to be authentic and build rapport is with appropriate small talk. If you've spent time learning about the client, you can casually mention something in common like, "I noticed on your LinkedIn that you're a volunteer on the Phoenix Pickleball Association. I finally made four point zero a few weeks ago and I'm obsessed. Would love to play a round with you when I'm there."

- *Be straight*: Sometimes the given situation calls for a more direct approach. "Hey Bob. Yes, this is a sales call!" This will typically get a brief chuckle. "Listen I only need a few minutes and I promise I won't sell you any encyclopedias or a new vacuum (he's definitely laughing now). I'd like to give you just a brief overview of how we're streamlining lead response and increasing call rates with companies like yours." This will typically get you your three minutes. Then be brief.

- *Ask for help*: "I was hoping you could help me with something." This is a great opener and appeals to their ego.

Etiquette: The Mark Quigley

Mark Quigley was a junior salesman with scant success to his name and didn't last long at our firm. But more than 35 years later, his legacy lives on.

Business dinners are a well-worn terrain for salespeople, a chance to break bread with clients or vendors. The system in our industry is clear. Our vendor partners—manufacturers whose products we sell—come to Canada and our territories throughout the United States to spend a day or two with sales reps showing them the ropes. They typically fly into town and pay to stay in a hotel, and the sales company will step up by picking them up and dropping off the reps at the airport, driving them to see customers, and feeding them.

The reps occasionally pick up the odd meal on their trip (they'll insist), but usually, given the travel expenses, the host pays for meals. We will typically have at least one meal per week with vendors or customers, or both. The senior-most person in our sales firm usually pays the bill when we're picking up the tab, and it's typical to take more than one company employee along in order to fill some chairs.

On the day in question, we went to a nice Italian restaurant in Toronto, and we started ordering our meals. The vendor picked chicken parmesan ($26) and a side salad ($8). The owner ordered the same thing. It came to me, and I chose the blackened tilapia with rice ($24) and a side salad. Albert—of the Albert Martin demo fame—ordered pasta Bolognese ($22) and a Caesar salad ($10).

Next, it was Mark Quigley's turn to order. "Hmm. Let's see," he said. "I'll have the surf and turf ($46) and a Caesar salad. No, wait, let's go with the tableside Caesar for two ($24). Hey, Albert, are you good to change out your Caesar for tableside? The waiter will prepare it for us from scratch right at the table."

"Uh, ok, I guess that's fine," Albert said, confused.

I hadn't entirely closed my menu, so I glanced at the prices to discover that Mark had not only ordered the most expensive meal, he'd also ordered the most elaborate starter, in addition to an expensive scotch before dinner. After dinner, he ordered the most expensive dessert and the fanciest coffee, too.

And this was from the most junior guy on our team.

At my next dinner with Quigley, he pulled the same stunt, again ordering the most expensive item on the menu. It kept happening again and again. It didn't matter what type of food we were eating, whether it was Japanese, Chinese, Mexican, Parisian, English. Every single time, Mark would order the most expensive thing.

After witnessing this a few times, Albert and I talked about it, and he was just as outraged and embarrassed as I was. As Quigley's expensive orders continued, I'd glance at the menu and whisper in Albert's ear. "Looks like it'll be the surf and turf again tonight, eh?" The next time, Albert beat me to it with his guess.

It became a standing joke. And several other people in the company began to copy that behavior. Whenever anyone (who isn't the host) orders anything at or near the top price on the menu, we'll joke and say, "Doin' a Quigley, eh?"

I can laugh about the story now, but experiencing it was painful, especially given how I was raised. I was taught to never order the most expensive thing, especially when someone else is paying the bill. You can get a moderately-priced item and show some common sense decency when you're ordering. This is why we regularly teach our sales team not to make the same mistake as Mark Quigley, especially if suppliers are paying.

So, having learned how much people do notice—and in an attempt to avoid pulling a Quigley—I took it upon myself to learn these essential etiquette tips when dining out with business associates:

- **Arrive on time:** As we say here, "Arriving early is on time, and on time is late." It's common sense to arrive a few minutes ahead and get the lay of the land. You can let the staff know you're there and attend to any issues. You also get the added benefit of getting the best seat at the table. I find the best place to sit is dead center in a table with my back to the wall. This provides a prime view of the restaurant and allows access to all conversations. If you sit at the head or end of the table you may be stuck with limited conversation.

- **Dress appropriately:** Again, common sense prevails. Gauge the crowd and venue and dress based on the occasion and the type of restaurant. Silence your phone and put it away.

- **Cutlery:** My mom was always quick to remind me of the cutlery order. The standard is to use the utensils on the outside first and work your way in for different meal courses. Your salad fork is on the outside of your entree fork. It's a smaller fork and should only be used for salad. Use the larger fork for your main dish. Your water glass is on the left-hand side of your wine glass.

- **Wait until everyone gets their meal:** It's polite to wait to start eating until everyone has their meal. If you're at a pub-style venue where random foods arrive at various times, or if your host insists that you start eating, then feel free to take a few small bites until they get their meal.

- **Be kind to your server:** How many times have you heard the story about the woman who dumped this seemingly awesome guy after they went on a date at a restaurant only to witness him being rude and condescending to the staff? Use "please" and "thank you" and always tip generously. Typically, in North America, 20% is the standard gratuity. Trust me, people will glance and try to see what you're tipping.

- **Be mindful of what you order:** Follow your host's lead and pick something mid-priced on the menu or in lockstep with your host. Also, if the host is drinking water, don't order a drink. Another tip is when ordering your meal, choose something that you can easily eat with a fork. Never order anything you have to touch with your hands, since these items can be pretty messy. I also try to avoid red sauce or anything that can splash and stain my shirt.

- **Proper serviette (napkin) use:** The rule is once your napkin hits your lap where it belongs, it should never rise above the table again unless you are holding it and using it for discretely wiping food off your face and hands. When you get up to use the restroom, place it on your chair. When you sit back down, place it immediately back in your lap and leave it there. When done eating and getting up from the table do the same thing.

- **Show gratitude:** Be sure to thank your host for inviting you and for the meal and make parting comments with others at the table. Exchange contact information and business cards if appropriate.

- **The bottom line:** If you follow these tips, they will help you succeed in other areas, too. After all, you only get forever to make another impression, and you don't want to be forever known as the underperforming salesperson eating like a king. Order the surf and turf at your discretion, but don't be surprised by your colleagues' whispering about the next Mark Quigley.

CHAPTER 9

SITTING IS NOT SELLING

I've heard the excuse 1,000 times from 100 reps.

"Are you going out on calls today?" I ask.

"No, this is my office clean-up day," they'll say, as though their office work is some sacrosanct privilege.

While there are certainly things salespeople are required to do in the office such as popping in to fill out forms, I challenge the idea of office days. These represent days off for a rep. They weren't hired to sit in the office, and the last thing I want them doing at their target earning level is clerical work. If you don't set and attend calls every day, you're not selling.

This came to me in a flash one day when I was interviewing reps. "Tell me about a typical week in your job now. Walk me through last week or the week before so I can understand how many calls you make and work pattern." Usually I'm shocked at how many say the same thing and set a horrible trap for themselves.

"I'm usually on the road two or three days per week and the other two days in the office," they tell me.

"Oh, how's that broken up?"

"Well, I usually have Mondays and Fridays in the office to clean up from my time in the field."

Busted.

If I say, "Well, if you spend Friday cleaning up from the week, what's there left to do on Monday?" they usually gulp and respond, "Oh no, I meant to say Friday is for a cleanup and Monday is for planning and prospecting for the coming week."

What I hear is this rep is programmed to sit in the office, chat at the water cooler, flirt with Rosie the new admin, and generally slack off for two of five work days. In other words, they're taking a four-day weekend every week from their true role which is to visit customers. Anything in the way of being in front of customers every day is a distraction. With 40% of selling days wasted, they're probably running at 50% sitting versus selling, which is unacceptable.

If you have a 40% to 50% workload in the office to cover your territory you're not a sales rep. I coach salespeople to consider approaching their job differently and think of the office as a pit stop, not a destination.

At my firm, we don't provide cubicles or offices for salespeople. There's one room with a desk surface that wraps around the entire room save for one corner, and there we have a small huddle table. There's room for two to three reps to clear up paperwork or schedule appointments. It's not made to be comfortable. There are also other cubicles they can borrow for an hour or so for the same purpose. We used to say, "Never provide a comfortable chair for a salesperson or they'll spend all day in it."

I train the salespeople to ensure they're visiting at least one client every day. The argument I get invariably is, "I need Friday to clean up from everything, and I need Monday to set appointments for the following week." As you work through other chapters in this book, and in the example scenario below, you'll see how this can become unnecessary.

In the 80/20 chapter, you'll remember I'm not just visiting my 80— I'm looking for my competitors' 80 and chipping away at it, all the while circling around those larger accounts to find "feeder" accounts that are spin-offs or supporting companies. For instance, around the Ford plant in

Oakville, there are hundreds of plants that support them with auto parts, chemicals, paints, supplies, and safety gear.

Let's say it's Tuesday and you're visiting an account where MajorTech, a major electronics manufacturer, is supporting them with PCB testing services. Many companies make their living off MajorTech. You not only want to target MajorTech, but you want to work concentric circles around them, finding every interrelated company.

You showed up that day with a demo and donuts to treat the workers, and after a productive meeting, you plan to drop on by the following Monday to pick up the demo gear to ship to another rep. Using your best friend Google and the local city's technology directory, you scour the area for accounts. You find a company called Acme Tech Solutions a couple of streets away, and using LinkedIn in your car, you find names, connect to your ZoomInfo account for full details, and give Larry, the VP of engineering, a call from the car. You ask if he can pop down to the lobby to meet you.

"Next time," he says, giving you two better names and what they do.

Two days later, on Thursday, you hit the lobby of MajorTech to check on the demo and reconnect with George, who you interacted with previously. You pass over the specs and offer any needed clarifications. Then comes the killer line. "Look, George, while I'm here, I need to check on the demo and make sure it's working ok for you guys. Could you pop me back to the lab to check on it?" Of course, this is bold, but you've already established credibility, and most of the time it works.

We head back to the lab, and the unit is sitting there, lonely, with two days of dust. Typically, most people don't touch the demo until the last block of time allotted to them. Being proactive reinforces their need to start evaluating the unit today before it's too late. When Monday comes, you've created a situation that allows you to visit MajorTech to pick up the demo unit and stop by Acme Tech Solutions. Your due diligence last week is making your next week more productive. Monday is already filling up with sales opportunities, and you don't even have time to go to the office.

Always Ask for a Mini Tour

While you're engaged with a new customer asking probing questions and learning about their business, always be sure to ask this simple question: "Hey, could you give me a mini-tour of your facility?" Then be quiet and see if they comply.

They will either say yes or no, but make sure once you pose the question you let it hang until they reply. If he or she continues to hem and haw for a few seconds throw in the line, "Look, I promise I won't sell anyone any encyclopedias or vacuums."

During the mini-tour you'll learn new things about their business, including what they make, production methods, equipment, and information about their customers. A mini-tour will show you everything they're not buying from you. And it could provide clues and research to help you uncover an advantage.

Facts and Figures on Selling

Here are few facts and figures I've collected about selling, prospecting, and cold calling. None of this is scientifically proven, but as I like to say, "Hear me now, believe me later."

- The best time to cold call is between four and five p.m. or eight and nine a.m.

- It takes an average of seven to eight cold call attempts to reach a prospect.

- If you're going to sit in the office to prospect, Thursday is the best day.

- Half of all sales go to the sales rep that responds first.

- Every sale will take five to seven follow-ups after the meeting.

- Half of all sales reps give up after one follow-up.

- Most decisions to buy in medium-sized companies are done by only half a dozen people. Figure out who they are.

- LinkedIn is now your best friend for prospecting. ZoomInfo is your next best friend.

- You need to ask for referrals. If you do, most of the time you'll get them. Most salespeople never ask for referrals.

- Customers will trust you more and prefer you if you came by way of a referral.

- Learn the rules of empathy. It's the key to having customers believe you understand their needs.

- Train, train, train, and always follow the greed-based learning (GBL) factor.

- Customers are lost every year. Never stop touching base and keep them current.

- Always tell great stories in your presentation and remember to focus on the first three minutes.

- Most customers prefer to be called (via phone).

- If you can't book time with the ideal contact, visit the buyer.

- You need to follow up leads fast. One hour is maximum and three to five minutes is ideal.

- Social media doesn't sell for you, it confirms their decisions.

- Companies with good social media come across as more trustworthy.

- The company president should drive the social media messaging

- Negative reviews will kill you. Solve every problem completely every time.

Pessimism Will Affect Your Creativity

Is the glass half-full or half-empty?

If you're feeling pessimistic, you'll tend to view the glass as half-empty. Creativity, and more importantly, productivity, can be decimated during periods of pessimism. Periods of pessimism even happen to eternal optimists.

Pessimism and optimism frame the way we view benefits, opportunities, and challenges along with missed chances, failures, and problems. I've developed a thesis that everyone operates somewhere on the miserable continuum.

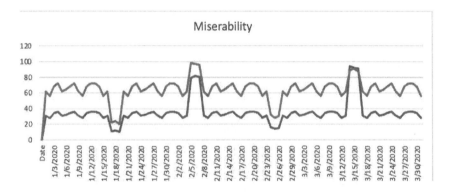

The chart above, created by Dr. Glenn Poulos (not a real doctor but a legend in his own mind), shows how everyone operates at their own base level of miserability. Some people seem eternally happy. Notice Sally indicated in the orange series operates at a base level of between 60 and 70, while Bob in blue is much lower. They can both have spikes up and down but notice they never reach 100% optimism or zero percent optimism. The spikes Bob receives to the upside (such as winning a huge deal) are much larger than those afforded Sally, and Sally's lows take her down much lower in proportion than the lows for Bob.

This is not science, but rather a metaphor for managing optimism. The first is to identify and label your standing self on the miserability index. Are you a 30, 50, or an 80? Our base level is formed from our experiences as we go through life. It's possible to move your base level, but not without keen introspection and work on yourself. For instance, a divorce for me moved me a full 20 points lower on the scale, and it took five years of hard work to regain my former level.

Here are some of the problems you can encounter if you don't monitor your pessimism and work to improve it.

Pessimism Destroys Creativity

Pessimism is like a quiet killer, creating a toxic bubble around you while affecting others who deal with you. Just as a rising tide lifts all boats, so does the ebb tide ground everyone in its wake. While pessimistic, you'll be communicating in negative ways and undermining your own creativity as well as those around you. You'll blame yourself and in time, you'll develop a "why bother?" attitude, becoming more reluctant to try the next time something else goes wrong. This is why it's vital you identify these tendencies and work on yourself, your attitudes, and your behavior.

Pessimism Destroys Your Well-being

People who harbor a more pessimistic outlook tend to have lower social support, lower resilience, lower ability to cope with stress, and a greater propensity for depression and anxiety disorders.[17] Negative thinking not only causes stress, it also can increase your risk of a heart attack and other serious health problems.[18] It's safe to say, *your shitty attitude may be killing you.*

Pessimism is Demotivating

When your heart is not in it, your performance suffers, and as I point

---

17 Markus Zenger, Heide Glaesmer, Michael Höckel, and Andreas Hinz, "Pessimism Predicts Anxiety, Depression and Quality of Life in Female Cancer Patients," *Japanese Journal of Clinical Oncology* 41, no. 1 (September 6, 2010), https://doi.org/10.1093/jjco/hyq168.

18 John B. Whitfield, Gu Zhu, J. George Landers & Nicholas G. Martin, "Pessimism is associated with greater all-cause and cardiovascular mortality, but optimism is not protective," Scientific Reports, July 28, 2020, https://www.nature.com/articles/s41598-020-69388-y.

out in *you only get forever to make another impression*, your boss is always watching and noticing everything! Negative thoughts will demotivate you and affect your job performance.

It's Bad for Your Relationships

Perception is reality, and when you spend all day thinking the worst, you'll turn people off and drive them away. People will avoid you and start to look for excuses to be someplace else.

Years ago, back in the late 1990s, I worked with a manager who was both a technical whiz and an incredible salesperson. As the company grew, he took on management duties in one of the sales groups with four to five salespeople reporting to him. This turned out to be one of my most difficult moments to manage in my career, and I still reflect on those days wondering what he and I could have done better.

It started with me overhearing watercooler comments from his team in a harsh tone and heavy-handed approach. There's truth to the myth that great salespeople don't make great managers. I've heard numbers that only one out of six or seven salespeople are suited to the role.

The problems with this manager were deep-rooted. Most of his reports were keen to ask him for advice, and he was generous in offering it. He was highly skilled in situation and politics evaluation, and came from a position of strength on behalf of the company.

However, what often happened was the salespeople would flip the script and put themselves in the role of customer advocate. Essentially, he would spend time explaining how to win the deal at a decent profit for the company while maintaining standard terms and conditions. The sales team members would capitulate, wrangle, and manipulate on behalf of the customer, and in short, ignore everything the manager said.

As the situation unfolded over time, the manager grew pessimistic about his duties and control of the staff.

"They never listen to me, so why do I even bother?" he would often say. His pessimism also caused him to drift down on the *miserability index* to an unhealthy level. He would often begin with a strong will, want to move up the spectrum, and act positively. But as he felt challenged and ignored, his mood would sour and his tone would become harsh, critical, and almost impossible to tolerate. His entire message would become lost as he grew more frustrated. People began to avoid the manager even when his input was needed, and they would try to navigate approvals with the least interaction possible. At meetings, the reps would either remain silent on issues or say everything was perfect, often choosing not to mention huge new opportunities out of fear of confrontation.

At the same time, the spirit of this highly-valued sales manager was being drained, and his creativity became bottled up. He ultimately asked to be removed from these duties and go back to focusing on direct sales to customers, which allowed him to slowly get his spirit back. However, could he have handled his reports challenging his direction in such a way that they remained motivated and he didn't feel disrespected?

There are numerous tips and techniques I use as a sales manager to handle difficult-to-manage salespeople. Since much of this person's pessimism came from a lack of cooperation from the staff, I would encourage changing tactics with the same goals in mind, explaining how to win the deal at a decent profit for the company while maintaining our standard terms and conditions. Some of these include:

1. **Discussing the strategy and then following up with a quick note to ensure clarity.** "Hey Bob, thanks for your time discussing the project you're close to closing at Acme Tech. I'm glad we were able to agree on a strategy. For clarity, here are the steps and objectives we need to follow:

   a. Drop by personally this week and see how the demo is going. Tell them it's in high demand and you need to pull it on Monday. Be sure to visit both times.

   b. Ensure they're aware that to meet the timelines the units will need air freight from the factory in Malaysia, and we'll need to quote them on that (typically it's about $1,200 per unit). Otherwise, we'll ship them by sea and they're looking at 12 weeks total.

c. Given the engineers will ask for price concessions and you'll have a second round with the buyer ensure you quote list. Stick to the plan of offering two percent for the expected quantity to the engineering team if they push you and we will save three percent for the buyer.

2. **Refocus.** Often, salespeople will balk at all my techniques. They'll say, "Something in my hand something in my mind. That's old school, Glenn. I can't get through to the buyers." I'll offer them the advice. "You raise a good point. I know it's difficult at times to get through to the decision makers, but let's pause and refocus and see if we can circle back to how you create interest once you do get through to them."

3. **Boomerang.** When the salesperson is being stubborn and offer sticking points, I will turn the issue back on them and say, "Hey, great point. Do you have any ideas about that?"

4. **Defer.** Often times, salespeople are just being difficult and will bring up discretionary issues as they attempt to deflect being managed. When they get sidetracked like this and I'm working on having them take in a specific strategy I will say, "Look, I understand your concerns about the CRM and getting quotes out in a timely manner, but let's cover that in the weekly L-10 meeting."

5. **Backhanded challenge.** "Hey Barry, I was wondering if anything was bothering you yesterday. I noticed that when I was going over the new three-three-three strategy you seemed agitated and almost annoyed. Is there something we need to discuss?"

6. **Point out the negative effects.** "Hey Tony, you may be seemingly getting your point across, but your delivery is so harsh. The people

listening are not actually agreeing with you. They're capitulating so you'll stop talking. They're actually tuning you out and don't care whether you're right or wrong."

7. **Point out the positive effects.** "Hey Taylor, did you notice during networking and strategy session yesterday you were able to inspire consensus and agreement by allowing everyone the freedom to express their opinion without harsh judgement? When they're all made to feel part of the idea and strategy, there's commitment and cooperation on the resulting plan."

If you're suffering with pessimism clouding your judgment and affecting your behavior, I suggest you try the following:

Uncover the Source of the Pain

Typically, attitudes that have shifted over time or, as noted above, shifted down on the miserability index are usually related to some specific root experiences that have caused this pain. You should identify the feelings you have concerning these experiences. I often recommend and offer support (financially) and encourage people to:

- Learn meditation to help clarify the issues and isolate the source of our negative self-talk.

- Seek professional help from a therapist. I've often offered to cover three to six months beyond basic benefit coverage to ensure they don't avoid this for financial reasons.

Be Honest

Once you have had the epiphany that "Hey, I think I am being a jerk or negative or pessimistic," you have made a huge step. Solve this problem by changing your mindset to be more optimistic or by reliving positive examples and stories.

Take Healthy Steps to Break the Cycle

Get help, seek counseling, and realize pessimism is a slow and deadly killer. It will suck you dry of ambition and leave you depressed and defeated. If you can hit the problem head on and find out what experiences shaped your pessimistic outlook, you can start the process of reframing your outlook and changing the course of your life.

CHAPTER 10

RAPPORT BUILDING

I have a basket of rapport building questions I can reach into when I need to break the ice with new customers or enhance the relationship with pre-existing ones. However, rather than just throw a bunch of questions at you, let's delve into the subtleties of rapport and how to build it with people. This really is key to what comes with rapport—and that is *trust*.

First, you need to feel worthy of someone else's time. Early in my career, I used to struggle with this, as I saw so many customers who were older or in more senior positions as better than me. I felt unworthy to take up their time, as though I didn't deserve to talk to them.

I had to shake things up with myself and realize my own worth. This takes time, practice, and in some cases a leap of faith. But make no mistake, this step is crucial. Realize that you are worthy by virtue of your existence. Accept this and shift your mindset to believe and live this mantra.

As you move to building rapport, I find the best way to start is to use questions that foster the answer to the query, "Tell me about yourself?" These could include questions such as:

- Do you have any kids or pets?

- How long have you worked here?

- What's on your bucket list?

- Where did you grow up?

Second, look for areas of *shared humanity*. At the end of the day, we are all the same. We all put our pants on one leg at a time. You need to keep that in mind and treat each customer with the same dignity and respect we all expect. You need to look past what they have or do not have and remember we are all the same while we ask some questions such as:

- What's something you're proud of accomplishing?

- If you became a teacher, what would you teach?

- If I invite you to my karaoke night, what's your go-to song?

- If I give you a free plane ticket, where would you go?

The next step is observed impressions, and I usually look for things about the other person that I can admire or appreciate. Find some common ground or an interest they have you can resonate with. There's always something and this is an excellent source of material for which you can build rapport, such as:

- What are you most grateful for?

- For what you would want to be remembered for?

- If you were to be an expert in something, what would it be?

- If you could change places with someone, who would you choose?

Moving on, I find extending questions to those around family will build strong rapport, but you need to seek cues that they have moved to a level with you they're willing to be open about such topics. I usually use pets as a starting to point test the waters. Tread slowly and make sure you're staying within bounds as you probe with questions such as:

- Are you an animal lover?

- Do you have any pets?

- Do you have siblings? How many? Where do you fit in the mix?

- How did you meet your husband/wife?

- Do you have children? How many? Boys/girls?

- Where did you grow up?

- Do you still have family there?

- Why did you move?

The last piece about rapport I want to touch on is telling the truth. It requires courage and a willingness to take a chance. But I can assure you, leaders and people in authority will sense it and appreciate it, and rapport will follow.

Bottled Water Rack Factor

I found myself at a career crossroads in the early 2000s. I ended up leaving the Japanese company on good terms, as it was a mutual decision to part ways. Over the course of nearly a decade, I grew the company from two million dollars to almost $50 million, and the company I left was much bigger and more developed than the company I joined. Still, it was the right time to move on.

I went back to my other company, and when I did, there was not a real home for me right away. I was the founder, owner and equal majority shareholder but my brother had been running the company with our other partner. There wasn't an easy opportunity to slide myself into a role like president or sales manager. I wasn't going to compromise someone's job just to give myself a title.

We decided to invest in a somewhat different business—a metal fabrication company that builds racks for bottled water machines in offices, like the five-gallon jugs that are popular in workplaces. You needed to store these water jugs somewhere, and we ended up manufacturing the bottle water racks to store them.

It was our first foray into manufacturing. And I went in with a catch-all role as a sort of president/chief cook and bottle-washer, no pun intended. The company didn't have any salespeople, and they definitely didn't need me to tell them how to bend steel and weld it together, as that wasn't my thing. They needed me to do things like find customers, build a website, and create marketing materials.

Despite the wide range of duties, my actual job was closer to director of sales and marketing. And since we didn't have a salesperson, I became the salesperson too. At the time, there were no smartphones and there wasn't a lot going on in terms of the internet. Calls were still made the old-fashioned way. Everybody made appointments and went and visited customers.

I found myself in an industry that I didn't know, selling a product that I was still learning, and with a company that was highly dependent on me. This felt as much like going back to square one as is possible. There were no leads and no phones ringing.

It was my time to take all of my factors and lessons, scrape together my pride, and get on the road to go and sell. There was a time at the very beginning where I was overcome with a sense of fear. *Oh my God, what have I gotten myself into?* But then, the next day, my lovely friend greed kicked in. Ah, greed. I got in my car and decided to visit the biggest water bottle company in Ontario. In fact, at the time it was the biggest in Canada. At the time, it was Crystal Springs, and they were huge. And they were right around the corner from my company's office. The other big regional water company was Culligan.

There was a very capable competitor in the same town as us building the same product that basically had all the business. We were mainly serving Ontario, which is fairly big, but at the time, there were a lot of bottled water companies and a lot of springs. Cedar Springs, Canada Springs, they all ended in Springs. Eventually, the big corporate powers of Nestlé and Coca-Cola and Pepsi bought up many of the water companies.

I put all my tools to the test. I showed up with something in my hand and something in my mind. I had a name that I knew, so I walked in the firm's office and asked for the contact. "Oh, he doesn't work here anymore. What do you want?" Not a great start, but I wasn't rattled.

"Well, we've got these great new portable water racks, and we're saving people a ton of money and serving bottled water better than it's ever been served before. And I just figured you guys want to get involved."

"Ok, well, our marketing team would handle that. They're at our office on Dixie Road, unit seven. There's no sign, just walk in the door."

So, I got back in my car, and I went straight over to Dixie Road, and as instructed, I walked right through the door and introduced myself to Mark, who I was told to ask for. "I'm here to get all your bottled water rack business," I said.

"Ok, well, sit down," Mark told me. We got to talking, and I started showing Mark our racks.

It didn't happen on the first day, but in short order things changed. I started getting orders from them and pretty soon, we had 100% of their business.

I went from being a senior executive at a $50 million company to starting over with a bruised ego, facing challenges I didn't know that I could accomplish. Yet, I still decided that I was going to get in my car and make a sales call. And once I started and realized, "Hey, I just knocked off the biggest water company in Canada," it was easy to go to the next one. In that moment, I flipped from being completely fucking miserable to happier than I'd ever been.

I was also pleasant in front of customers. When you're a sales guy, and that's your true job, and when you don't have all these other side jobs, it's the most rewarding thing you can do. From that point forward, I made a commitment to myself that I wasn't making any appointments for bottle water rack clients, I would just drop by. A lot of them were smaller companies that had an owner running the show. Instead of calling and bugging them, which wouldn't have been well received, I just started showing up.

I drove all over Ontario and found every company that ended with the words water or springs, and I visited every one of them. In short order we captured a lot of business really quick and pissed off that other guy in town.

In time, I hired a dedicated salesperson. I sat him in the car and told him the story of what I did. I drove him around showing him how to do exactly what I was doing. Eventually, I didn't have to get in the car with him anymore. He took over and did it himself. This allowed me to go back to running different parts of the business and handle my executive job functions.

While we didn't end up lasting very long, the experience taught me an important lesson about getting back to the basics of selling. I had everything pulled out from under me, and the only thing I could do was go and sell, and that opportunity was a gift. It took me back to the hunger I felt when I was in my early 20s. My skills hadn't diminished—if anything, I was sharper and more refined.

Sometimes, you've got these career salespeople who never want to become a manager, and they might be the smartest people in the company. For them, that's ok, especially if it's the freedom of the job that they're after.

Become your Customer's Top Sales Rep

One of the most powerful ways to build strong customer relationships is through reciprocity, or learning about your customer and finding ways to help them grow.

This is the real reason why I always ask for a mini tour. No, I don't actually want the tour to be mini, but I learned by adding the word mini it lowers the time expectation on the customer. I don't want them thinking *ugh, this guy is going to waste my whole morning.* Once we begin the tour, however, I find customers love talking about their company and what makes it great.

During the tour, I am jotting down notes (if appropriate) and making note of everyone I meet (as we covered in the callbook factor). My goal with the tour is to see how each department ticks and how the company operates. What works well? What the company is lacking? I encourage the customer to show me every nook and cranny of the building, from design and engineering to corporate, production, assembly, staging, testing, packaging and yes, even shipping.

Once you learn the ins and outs of how your customers make their products, you'll learn how they make money and can uncover opportunities to leverage more sales by learning about other potential customers you can approach.

An Example of Applying Reciprocity

I called a customer who manufactures parts to be installed in satellites. They bought a lot of test instruments, which is what I was selling at the time.

On our mini-tour, I was shown the calibration lab. We chatted briefly with the calibration manager, Lou, and with some gentle poking and prodding, he said they were closing the lab and farming out their work. Lou was retiring, and he was sad to see his baby being farmed out after years of keeping all of the company's gear in top shape.

From my visit with Lou, I garnered that the manufacturing company had started using ACME Calibrators, a service in Toronto 90 minutes away. I got this information from a label I saw on a cardboard shipping box. ACME Calibrators was a customer I could just never break into. They only bought used equipment and were as cheap as the day is long. I wished Lou well and made a mental note to send him a small token for his retirement. All the while, I was chomping at the bit thinking of the leverage this golden opportunity would offer me.

Weeks earlier, I'd been in the area looking for little gems of opportunity that most sales reps miss (20/80) and came across a start-up lab company. I called the lab manager I'd met once before.

"Hey Rick, I have what I think might be a great sales opportunity for your firm. Can you tell me who the vice president of sales is? I'd really like to engage with him on this." He quickly offered that Rafael was heading up sales and reported directly to the owner. I called him and he agreed to meet with me. Rick, the production test manager, also joined us, and the company president ended up entering the meeting room too.

I started to lay out the foundation of my plan.

"Look, I know you guys have some calibration equipment here and are already doing your own calibrations to lower overhead. Perhaps you could consider taking on this outside work, and since they have hundreds of instruments it could be quite lucrative for you," I told them.

I asked them to be discreet when approaching the manufacturing company and was sure to give Lou's name and a few other tips I'd picked up from my tour.

The VP was thrilled. Rick was glowing too, as it was "his guy" who brought them this opportunity. "What are we buying from Glenn, anyway?" the president asked.

"Well, we were looking at DynaMon Spectrum safety monitors, but we decided to go with more of the AlertMon units we got last year," Rick said.

"Oh," the president said. "Does the DynaMon do the job?"

"Well yes. In fact, quite well, but they're a tad more expensive and we were trying to trim costs."

"How much more?" the president asked.

"About five percent," I offered.

"Look, Glenn. This is quite out of the ordinary, and frankly, I am bit speechless," the president said. "We're in the start-up phase and cash flow is king for us right now. Leveraging our existing equipment for more cash flow and staff utilization is just genius, and what a great opportunity. How can I thank you in return?"

Blushing profusely and a bit choked up from his heartfelt message, I cracked a joke and said, "Well, normally I would ask for your firstborn but I already have five kids, so I'll tell you what. When you're at your CEO insiders club with your tech buddies, could you refer me to them and perhaps pass me a few names?"

"Damn straight I will," he said. "And I'll send you an email with them copied opening the door for you."

I thanked them for their time.

But I wasn't done acting as a facilitator. I immediately headed straight for Nano CaseCo, a transit case supplier in Mississauaga near the Pearson International Airport. I didn't have the volume required to get a direct deal with CaseCo—I was buying from a reseller with a slight markup. I resent this setup and was clamoring for a direct deal.

I laid out my idea to the VP of sales at CaseCo. I explained to him that I'd just visited both companies, and now after 20 years our first customer was going to be shipping hundreds of instruments around to get calibrated. They were going to need dozens of cases even if they rotated their use among models. I also explained the start-up I visited was now going to chase down this business. They also would need to ensure they had reliable shipping cases for the customers they would pursue as well. The VP was elated, and congratulated me for how well we were doing selling their cases. He was aware of the orders we'd sent to their reseller and said he was ecstatic about the huge deal.

"I'm going to call them myself and see about this opportunity, and if they decide to go with our cases, I'll be sure they come to you for purchase and set you up directly," he said.

"Thanks, that's incredible news," I said. "Listen, while the going is good, can I pick your brain? Can you think of any tech start-ups you've sold lately that I could target with our test instruments?" He offered me two or three names that I could use in my day-to-day prospecting.

Later that week, I got a call from Rick, the production test manager from the start-up.

"I have good news, great news, and unbelievably fantastic news for you. What do you want first?" he asked.

"Start at the bottom and work your way up," I said.

"Ok, well, we discreetly made inquiries with the company you referred us to and ultimately spoke to Lou's boss. We're quoting them on a calibration deal for almost 300 instruments a year!"

"Wow, that's amazing. And what's the great news?"

"The president was happy about the whole thing and mentioned how you kept mentioning that you and I worked together. He credited me for being the catalyst that brought it together and I got a spot bonus good enough to book a week's holiday for me and the wife to Cancun."

"Well, I can't wait to hear the unbelievable fantastic news," I replied.

"Obviously, we're cancelling the requisition for the AlertMon units and buying 10 of the DynaMon units from you. The president also recommended our parent company buy them and I would estimate they would need 40 to 50 units."

This is just one of many examples how asking for a mini tour might lead to myriad opportunities with the potential for big payoffs down the road.

My Mentor Made Me Do It

Imagine going home from work and telling your wife or husband, "Hey honey, I've decided to take the leap into sales. My salary will go from $80,000 to a $45,000 base salary plus the ability to earn up to $55,000 in commissions my first year, and unlimited ceiling on what I can earn going forward."

"What?" the spouse says. "You took a 50% pay cut for some sales job?"

"That's right sweetie, and I've never been more excited about a job in my life."

When you present an offer to someone that has a base plus commission component, or in our lingo, a fixed and variable portion, I believe about 90% of the recipients and their significant others fixate on what's guaranteed and struggle to consider the total target earnings (TE) potential. To give you an example, imagine I offer someone an $80,000 package with a 60% base ($48,000) and 40% variable (up to $32,000 in commissions). They're currently earning $58,000 as a system engineer.

At home, they discuss the job offer with their partner, but the spouse can't get past the base since it's a few thousand a year less than their current base salary. Despite explaining to them that their earnings potential would increase $20,000 or more, they're dead-set on increasing their base salary. So, I revise the offer with an increase in base pay, but their commission quota is cut in half. The rep doesn't mind—in fact, they smile from ear to ear.

So, imagine the leap of faith required for someone to make a jump from driving a forklift in the warehouse for $45,000 per year to a sales job with a base of only $36,000? This is one example of how mentoring is so powerful.

At one of my firms, we had a guy named Steve who did miscellaneous tasks for us like product inspections, testing, and driving the forklift. He was in his mid-20s and didn't have a post-secondary education. In fact, he hadn't finished high school either, and was working on his GED. This didn't prevent him from being a quick study, however.

At first, he was a pure warehouse guy packing boxes and moving skids around. But in time he began to stand out—particularly when we did special services for some customers. So we trained him to do special testing and reporting on a large upcoming project that evolved into minor repairs and tweaks to some items to ensure they were in spec before they shipped out. He did this job for almost five years, and in that time we came to learn he was a sponge when it came to cars and anything else he was passionate about, which turned out to be a lot of things.

In my daily trips around the building, I learned that Steve really wanted *more*. That *more* included more money, but he also wanted more challenge, flexibility, opportunity, and acknowledgement. Far more than he was going to get with us driving a forklift. Given his ability to ramble on incessantly about cars and learn more than I could ever imagine doing, I suggested he take a leap of faith and go into sales. This had him gob smacked at first.

"I could never sell anything. I wouldn't be any good at that," he said.

"Listen, Steve," I told him. "Every day you present products to people when you talk about cars. Just imagine the person paying you for the car you're describing once you're done."

Over time I continued to mentor Steve, and most days I would check in and spend a few minutes chatting with him. I began to share all these same stories, lessons, and tips you're reading now. Over and over, I would remind him the importance of following the plan and to make the calls, show up, know your shit, and be easy to do business with.

Soon we were at the point where he was ready to launch and needed to get a job in sales. He'd decided car sales would be best, and he started earmarking dealers in the city near Toronto where he lived and what cars they sold. Using GBL, he began learning everything he needed to know on all the cars and I primed him on how to get the job. Given the jump from warehouse to car showroom, he was going to need to take a leap of faith and go all in with "the secret" and imagine the life he wanted to live. As they say, anything the mind can conceive and believe, it can achieve. So, he needed to think, act, talk, and walk like he sold cars with the self-assured-ness most successful car salespeople portray.

"Forget emailing resumes or answering ads. Forget the phone. At face value you're not qualified, so you need to *sell* them on *you*," I told him. "You need to show up dressed like a car salesman, well-groomed and with a resume in hand. Walk in the front door and ask for the sales manager. If he's not there ask for the owner. When the manager comes out, remember to *never sit in the lobby* and look him straight in the eye and introduce your-self as you shake his hand. With the other hand, pass him the resume and say, 'Hey John, great to meet you. My name is Steve. I'm here to sell some cars for you.' And then shut up and don't say anything. He'll probably be wondering who the heck is he? Did I hire this guy, did someone else? What does he mean sell cars for me? Then at just the right moment, chuckle and say, 'Nah, I'm just kidding. I have a couple offers to sell for other dealers in the area, but I really want to sell Mazdas. When can I start?'"

He went from one dealership to another and made this speech his own. He adapted the language to what he was comfortable saying and visited 10 dealerships. He brought back nine stories of the interaction and had one job offer. I then proceeded to work through each exchange and coach him on what a 20-year veteran would do in each of the cases. I prepped him with a ton of responses and behaviors explained to him about intermittent reinforcement. He followed up the next day, and then on third day I had him visit those at the top of his list and say, "So, are you ready for me to move some cars for you?"

I also helped him talk over the job offer he received. In the end, I had him doing everything a seasoned rep would do and helped him break through fears some people never challenge. He got three more offers and ended up selecting his favorite brand. In his second month, he sold six cars. Ultimately, he learned a lot about the business of car sales and after talking over the challenges of that industry, I suggested he sell something in a more industrial capacity where he could get a car allowance, benefits, and more compelling environment. He made the jump and is now a well-seasoned rep selling high tech products and making more money than he thought possible.

Steve's success proved to me how much latent talent is inside our co-workers and friends, and how, with proper mentoring and coaching, they can make huge leaps in job duties, income, and satisfaction. When they ask how you did it, you can say," My mentor made me do it!"

CHAPTER 11

ERIK VOCKER'S ROCK

At the time, I was working for the Japanese electronic instrument manufacturer and was in charge of sales for Canada. This was the run-up to the late 1990s tech bubble, and electronics in Canada were booming, with much of it on the backs of Nortel.

I had to hire a new junior sales rep for my other company and approached a small community college with an engineering program to uncover graduates who were interested in a career in sales. While we often hired grads right out of college with much success, this has not always been the case. There was one of the graduating students, Erik Vocker, who seemed polished and asked sharp questions during my meeting with the students.

I ended up hiring Erik for a junior sales role. In this company, we called ourselves reps, and bought and sold products from manufacturers all over North America and Europe. Not too long after Erik started working for us, we sent him for a multi-day training session in Colorado, and he went a little bit early and stayed a little bit late to see the sights in Colorado. While he was there, I got a call from the company president of the firm we were representing.

"Who's this fucking Erik Vocker guy you sent down here? He's giving me the third degree about our contract together. What business does a junior sales rep I understand you hired two weeks ago have asking me about private legal documents between our two firms?"

"What?" I said, shocked.

"He wants to see the contract and check the terms. For fuck's sake, Glenn, I've never met a more nosy pissant in my life. I don't like him."

"You've gotta be kidding me," I said sheepishly.

I couldn't believe how nosey Erik was. I would never dream of thinking of asking such a thing. There's bold, and there's Erik Vocker bold. Erik was just out of school, and here he was trying to school the executives, demanding all these facts and figures that made all of us feel super uncomfortable. This was the founding director of a $100 million company and we were still making our way establishing our relationship with them. This was not someone Erik had the authority to question—especially not in this subject area.

While I thought his inquisitive and bold nature was initially a strength of Erik's, as it turned out, this was in fact a major liability. His behavior forced me to admit to myself the first red flag I saw in Erik, one that I initially overlooked when I was speaking to him and other students from his college. When I went in and shared I was the President of Anritsu Electronics Ltd., a subsidiary of a Japanese electronics company. I explained all the great things afforded candidates who pursued a job in sales and as the talk wore on, I asked for a show of hands on who would want to be considered for a role in sales. Over half the group put up their hand. I said I was going to give everyone 30 seconds to introduce themselves by name and why I should consider them for the job, and, in the end, I would send a list of who the successful candidates were and setup actual interviews.

When I concluded my talk and opened the floor for questions, the first hand that went up was Erik Vocker's. "So you're the President of Anritsu Canada, correct?" he asked.

"Yes," I said curiously. "Well, tell me, Glenn. Given you're only 32, is it a really small company, or is your title just overstated?" *OMFG,* I thought to myself, *did he just ask me that?*

"Neither," I said. "I merged a multi-million dollar business in with their firm a year ago, and I can assure you it's neither small nor overstated."

I hired Erik thinking his bold nature would be a great fit for sales. But by the time he was flying back from Colorado, I was so pissed off at him (and myself) I could barely contain myself.

When Erik came back, I was pretty much ready to fire him, but wanted to give him a chance to explain himself and see if things could blow over. Maybe he would show me something, tell me something, or offer something to make me change my mind. I was praying I wouldn't have to restart the hiring process all over again.

He showed me something, all right. Erik defended his demeanor toward the company president and continued with his interrogating ways during our debrief. He was also absolutely obsessed with a color photo of himself, he had had taken on the top of this mountain in Colorado. In the background of the photo, you can see the mountain, and in the foreground of the photo, Erik was holding a rock. This rock is the exact same shape of the mountain behind him.

I admit the photo was outrageously original and unique, and would at any other time impressed me with its ingenuity. But not today. I was fuming mad. So, between his shitty attitude and the stupid picture, I'd had enough. I ended up firing him that day. I don't report to or answer to a junior underling. I certainly wasn't going to report to Erik Vocker.

The magic of Erik doesn't end there. I was still upset over my bad hiring and Erik's outrageous behavior and attitude a couple of days later when, lo and behold, a box arrived that was shipped via FedEx all the way from Colorado. And it was *heavy.* It was addressed to Erik Vocker. He got *my* account number, and upon opening the large box, realized he'd FedEx'd himself the rock from the picture.

Bad Salespeople are Expensive (and Good Ones are Free)

In my haste of firing the rock collector Erik Vocker, I didn't restart the recruiting process like I should have. Instead, I went down the list of other candidates I had when I hired Erik and offered the job to someone I ranked lower on the list named Craig.

Craig turned out to be a quick study. He spoke well and could handle the products and presentation. There weren't any obvious red flags. He began making calls, and for a time, things were quiet. But then one fateful morning my phone rang. I recognized the number—it was a customer I had handled since I started in sales in the mid-1980s.

This was a customer I'd visited hundreds and hundreds of times. When I think of the callbook factor, sitting in the parking lot going over names, this is one of the customers I would always picture in my mind. The call was from the main receptionist, Jennifer.

"Glenn, we need you to come down here. We need to speak to you," she said.

I didn't question her with what or why, I just piled in my car and raced down the highway. I was reticent giving them up in the first place, but at that point I was in charge of running sales and the business. I arrived in the parking lot without a thought to my usual *factors*. There was no time for me to run the callbook factor and scour names in the directory, and I sure as heck didn't stop at Timmy's for a 12-pack of donuts. I marched in and approached Jennifer. I could see from her expression that this was something serious.

"Hi Glenn, thank you for coming so quickly. Can you please join me in the meeting room?" she said as she posted a *Be Right Back* sign on the desk with a number to call for service. She led me to a nearby meeting room, and to my surprise there was another receptionist in the room named Becky who filled in for Jennifer on her breaks and time off.

Someone else was there, too—a guy with the word *security* written on his shirt just over the breast pocket. I tried to maintain my composure, but I'm not one to have issues with security. At this point I was worried and wondering what in the hell was going on.

"Thanks again for coming, Glenn. I'm sorry to be meeting under these circumstances," Jennifer told me. "I asked Becky to join and security is sitting in as well."

"Ok," I offer meekly. "How can I help?"

"Well, Glenn, we've worked with you for years and years. You're a joy to deal with. We have often spoken of how thoughtful you are and quick to offer nice gestures and a box of donuts now and then. We were a bit sad when you were replaced with Erik, but he was professional if not a bit pushy. It must not have worked out with him because he was replaced with Craig."

"Uh-huh, that's correct," I said gulping.

Jennifer continued. "It started fine, Glenn, but we are here to advise you that Craig is never allowed back in this building, and if we see him within 100 feet of the building, we will call the police and likely ask your firm to never call on us again."

"Oh my God, Jennifer, what happened?" I started using my best active listening.

"Well, Glenn, Craig is a creep. He has taken to just showing up here without any appointments and with no one to see. He comes to speak to me and Becky. Yesterday, Becky was at the desk and he said to her, 'Becky, I'd really like to spend some time with you outside of work. I just graduated from a course called "How to Make Love to a Woman," and I really want to show you what I've learned.' We were already creeped out by him and were getting ready to call you when this happened. Now, we're at an absolute breaking point."

"Oh my God, I don't know what to say. I'm going to deal with this immediately, and I promise you'll never see him again."

"Ok, thank you, Glenn. I hate to dump this on you. You've always been a pleasure to deal with and we're certain you'll handle it so we can put this to rest without any formal charges."

That word "charges" resonated in my head as I was walked quickly back to my car. One of my best customers was using the words "your company" and "charges" in the same sentence.

I was ashamed.

I was furious.

I was embarrassed.

I was worried sick.

As I was about to pull out and make the return trip to the office, a thought crossed my mind. *Holy shit, if he did this to Jennifer and Becky, what about Sandra at TechNova Core around the corner and AbleTech just off the highway?*

With no time to waste, I hit up both customers. My worries turned out to be justified. TechNova Core was preparing to phone the police on the guy, and it was a similar story at AbleTech. I was now bubbling with rage at Craig and kicking myself the whole way back as I knew I should have done better during the hiring process. When I got back to the office, I burst in and charged at Craig, shaking my first and pointing in his face.

"You are so fucking fired, Craig," I told him. "You need to get the fuck out of here. Now!"

I was so apoplectic I couldn't even speak to him further and had him escorted out of the building. Safe to say, we never saw or heard from Craig ever again, but the damage was done.

Not all of my bad hires were rock senders or reception abusers, but I've had my share of bad hires and they all stick in my mind. Here are some of the pitfalls I've learned from hiring the wrong salesperson:

Time Killer

We all know how painful the early days of hiring a new direct report is. Regardless of their skills and success later, in the ramp-up, you will be investing a significant amount of time. If you discover that you've hired the wrong person, you can't recover this valuable time. Now you'll be behind from wasting time on the wrong hire, not to mention the time it will take to recruit and train all over again. In my experience, it usually takes about four weeks to recruit and hire a salesperson. There may also be time wasted by going back and trying to fix their mistakes with customers and colleagues. This is particularly bad for morale, especially when it could have been avoided.

Embarrassment

When you make a bad hire, there's no avoiding it. It reflects poorly on you and affects how people look at your skills. How often have you heard water cooler chatter like, "I just knew that new guy was no good. What kind of an idiot would hire him? To think, he's managing people here is scary." It can also be embarrassing for customers and force them to question your judgment.

Expensive

Time is one of the biggest costs associated with a bad hire, and as we all know, *time is money*. I use six to nine months of an employee's salary when guestimating the cost of getting it wrong. In my experience, that figure is actually low and somewhat conservative, given it sometimes takes months or even a year or more to pull the plug. In this scenario, the costs are now significantly higher.

Productivity Killer

Step back and think about all the other staff members associated with the onboarding process. Typically, all your top performers are required to spend time with the new guy, and during all this wasted time, they're not selling for you and their numbers can suffer as well. This can really hit the bottom line and escalate the costs of these unfortunate hiring mistakes.

Customer Impacts

We're often quick to remember how these bad hires affect those closest to us in the organization, and this can be a real trust killer. However, let's not overlook the significant impact this can have on your customers. That trust can often be impossible to win back, or can take years for those bad memories to fade, further escalating the time cost of a bad hire.

Employee Morale

Bad hires do not go unnoticed, and people love to talk about it at the water cooler. This bad news can often be shared on external review sites such as Glassdoor. This can affect future good hires, as negative reviews on Google reviews could lead to your next best hire turning down the job. As the saying goes, "Bad news reaches twice as many ears as good news."

Chain Reactions

All this bad news above can cause a snowball effect in your organization that leads to higher-than-expected turnover with good staff. It's clear you not only risk losing the person you just hired, but you also risk losing other valuable employees. This counts double if the bad hire was a manager. This leads to other managers needing to double down on coaching and training and causes others in the company to step up to pick up the slack—all of which leads to a hit in the bottom line.

Avoid Hiring Mistakes

If you want to minimize the number of hiring mistakes you make in the future, you need to get your recruiting process right:

- Define the type of candidate you need.
- Determine how their skills will need to mesh with company core values.
- Be slow to hire and quick to fire.
- Have a detailed interview process and reference checking system.
- Always watch for top sales talent. Top talent always have a job.
- Hire a professional sales recruiter.

I will say it again. Define your core values. Hire based on them and fired based on them.

I once had a staff member ask, "When do you fire someone, Glenn?" I always give the same answer. I wish I always took my own advice, but regardless, my answer is, "Jack, the time to fire someone is one minute, or as soon as humanly possible, after the very first time you think you should fire them. Trust me, it almost never gets better. That's what probation is for."

Hiring Erik and Craig taught me the importance of interviewing for the specific position, and ensuring that all the questions I ask are related to success in that role. I test them with questions that flush their attitude toward our core values. Another thing I do, too, is see if I have a shared connection—someone who knows this candidate outside of their listed references so I can ask for their thoughts. "We're thinking of interviewing this person," I'll tell the connection, and see what they say. It's another layer of security, one more chance to avoid hiring a bad salesperson.

Shut Up

I get it—you have the gift of gab, and you're genuinely *excited* to talk to customers. The products are the top of the line and you want everyone to know about them. But sometimes the best sales pitches are the ones you don't make.

The rules here are easy:

1. If you're talking more than a minute and you're not directly answering or asking a question, you're talking too much!

2. If you're talking more than 10% of the time, you're talking too much!

3. If you think you might be talking too much during your sales calls, you're talking too much!

Reasons you talk too much:

1. **Anxiety:** Words won't protect you. Letting the customer speak does not mean surrender. It's joining the winning side.

2. **You're poorly prepared:** Practice creating scripts, practice your scripts, role play, and stay on script.

3. **You're tired or stressed:** If you're tired or stressed, you're bound to ramble. Treat each call like you're an actor in movie. Leave your life in the car and stay in role. Get proper rest.

4. **Time management is not your strength:** Start on time, stay on point, be on time, and leave on time.

5. **Lack of humility:** You're the only one who loves the sound of your own voice.

6. **Lack of focus:** Stay on point and don't jump around from topic to topic.

CHAPTER 12

THE DAVID GLEASON FACTOR

In a Coke and Pepsi world, I was selling RC Cola.

My first job in sales, starting in 1986, was for a small specialty distributor of test and measurement gear from lines around the world. These companies hired other companies like mine that were typically in a country or region-specific exclusive area. The products required a face-to-face selling model and local in-country support but did not warrant a direct sales force. My employer's company was formed with 20 to 30 of these contracted relationships and had a team of sales and support staff across Canada. Having these 20 to 30 vendors gave the sales force a "tool bag" of T&M instruments sufficient to make quota in our sub territory. I covered Western Ontario.

While I wasn't selling the market leader, I knew my products worked better. My job was to identify market segments that might be consumers of the Cokes and Pepsis and then make them aware of our brand. This requires qualifying them for an upcoming need. Would they be in the market to purchase? Would they be willing to expand the search criteria and not just decide on buying the leading brand? Ultimately, I changed companies and learned why it's important to sell the number one and two brands.

Of course, our products were significantly more complicated than drinking a can of soda. We often shipped tens of thousands of dollars' worth of instruments, or perhaps even more than $100,000 for one instrument. Along with the hardware and costs of moving it around North America, we often had to have an applications engineer on staff or a small factory team for support on large sale opportunities.

The basic premise behind the David Gleason factor is rather simple. The customer drags you into the building, has you bring support staff and demo equipment, and makes all sorts of fanfare about your hardware. Your excitement level builds throughout the process and your manager keeps a close eye on the opportunity. After all, you're throwing all your resources at this deal. As the evaluation wears on you start to feel like you may finally be able to displace the incumbent, a top brand market leader that has dominated for years.

Your hardware is worthy and you carefully position all your strengths to show it in its best light. The customer asks you to leave the hardware for a two-week bake-off. Normally you wouldn't do this (see the demo factor) but given the magnitude of this opportunity, you discuss with the demo coordinator, your vendor liaison, and your boss, and you all agree this is the time to go all in. You offer to make the apps engineer available for any bake-off tests and provide any technical notes or bulletins. Before you know it, the two weeks have gone by and you call the customer.

"Can I drop by to pick up the demo and get an update from you, David?"

"No problem, Glenn. Come ASAP. We need to talk."

My heart pounds as I launch like a rocket to get myself in front of this customer. David Gleason is famous for his diatribes. He's known in the industry and famous for his business acumen and his incredibly deep pockets and amazingly short arms. He sits me down and explains how close the deal is going. In the end, they're leaning toward my product, but there is a problem: the price.

He's just not willing to pay virtually the same price for your product as the market leader. David is brutal. He's essentially offering to pay us 20%

off our stated price, but there isn't 20% in the margin chain on this level of instrument.

At this point, you unleash a veritable barrage of competitive bullets you've been studying since this ordeal began. Ultimately you capitulate and agree to fight for him to get him the best price. You take this back to the vendor and your boss and set up a conference call with David to reestablish the technical superior points that he graciously agrees to sit in on. Your best people from across the globe unleash a torrent of indisputable laser-focused technical points. David Gleason is consummate in his calm demeanor and says, "Guys, listen. I agree. You do have better specs here and there. Your display is nicer and has a better resolution. The point is, I've been using the other brand (the market leader) for 20 years. I'm sitting here thinking of switching sides, and as you know, there are five units at stake.

"But I cannot pay nearly the same price to switch from what I unquestionably assert is the market leader—my key supplier for 20 years. If you can't create a 15% to 20 % spread in this to make this worth my while, then I see no point in continuing with this charade."

My boss steps in. "Ok, David. I think we understand. As you know, Mr. Jones, the VP from the factory, along with myself, the owner of AlsoRan Tech distribution, commit to getting back to you with a compelling proposal. We appreciate your time and look forward to speaking with you soon." We start the process internally of exercising a ton of factors respectively on each other. We finally agree on five units and with a shared margin reduction we'll meet the 20% discount to upset the stranglehold market leader has had on this account. The bragging rights and reference points alone are worth millions.

I'm pumped and my excitement is uncontrollable. I craft a beautiful financial and technical proposal bound in Cerlox with a fancy cover and then proceed to hand deliver it so I can see the look on his face when he sees the deal we've put together. David Gleason is unavailable upon my arrival and I'm asked to leave my proposal. In fact, it takes me several weeks to finally get him on the phone. There was a period of time when I thought

I would never speak to him again. When I finally do speak to him he is bold, direct, and cheerful. The news he drops on me is like a bomb. He tells me without blinking an eye that he went ahead and purchased from the market leader. We lost the deal.

He tells me he was minutes from crafting a PO with our name on it, but when the VP of sales for the market leader hears this, he calls David and asks for a meeting. He agrees reluctantly because of their 20-year relationship. David explains that he's going with them, and is also saving 20% for a superior product. The market leader rarely discounts for anything other than early payment. He acts incredulous and shocked when he lets me know they countered our proposal with a 30% discount, free training, a three-year extended warranty, and platinum seats at the Montreal Forum for Habs vs. Boston. He thanks me for my time, and as he bolts out on his way to a meeting, he turns to me and says, "There's always next time."

The reality is now setting in and I seriously wanted to cry. David Gleason never ever wanted to buy our unit. It was all an elaborate stage act so he could drive the fear of God into the incumbent competitor who was being intransigent on the price, and it worked. He wanted to save a huge sum and get the units he wanted from the competitor, so he staged it all. He knew, given market share and brand value, in normal circumstances he could only beat them up for a few points at best. Further, they would probably be very tight with him on net 30-day payment terms, and he'd need to prove he could pay the bill on time because it was, after all, a half-million-dollar order.

David needed to cause a paradigm shift in the manufacturer, so he baited us into thinking we had a chance of winning the business. He pushed for a huge dog and pony show and no doubt probably had staff members friendly to the incumbent, feeding them with information on the investments we were making in demo gear and the staff we had to go on-site and do demos. The only way he could shift their mindset was to instill a very real fear that they were about to lose a huge account.

While he let our dog and pony show run wild, he played the next card in his hand flawlessly. We later learned he shut out the incumbent player and wouldn't speak to them. He let them stew and stress, and wonder and fester about how the trial of our gear was going. If only they could get in front of him and show the deficiencies in our unit they could turn the tables, save the order, and keep their margin as well. He let the whole charade play out and let us all play our parts.

The problem with having a Gleason pulled on you is the overall deceit perpetrated by the customer. In these cases, the customer is essentially lying to you. Naturally, they see this as a high-level negotiation tactic, but many salespeople get caught up in the song and dance show and lose sight of the big picture.

Nowadays, selling to large telecoms can also happen quite regularly. This same customer actually tried to pull the *double down David Gleason factor* on us. He came out of the woodwork again after not talking to us for a year and told us he needed to do another bake-off. The units in question were the latest models but functionally pretty much the same. At this point, we were definitely in the "once bitten twice shy" mode of operating and realized handily that despite whatever yarn he was spinning, he still wanted to maintain consistency in his test setups, and so we saved ourselves the time and money.

"Look David, we're convinced no matter what we do you'll still buy the other guy, so to save time let's make a deal," we said. "Let us know the price you need and we will bring our pricing in near that. Let's agree now we can't accept an order with that quote but you can use it as you see fit when talking to the other guys."

I don't recall the exact details, but I believe we brought our price down to near the spot they quoted last time. David was able to show them a competitor's quote and negotiate another 30% discount on five more systems! We followed the factor that it's better to be last than second and chose not to compete. We never sent in any staff or demos and were able to move on to other customers.

The Reverse David Gleason Factor

The Gleason factor lesson is burned into my experiences. I've told this story a hundred times over the years. Second only to the Gleason lesson is the lesson I called the *reverse Gleason*. This happened shortly after the first time I experienced the Gleason and even closer to the experience of the *double down David Gleason*. This was one of the most exciting moments in sales I have ever experienced. It was also one of the largest single one-time orders I have ever received of just over $1,000,000. I was serving as sales manager then and we were selling these $100,000 testers at a fast clip. This was the height of the telecom bubble.

It's important to set the stage and mental mindset we were in heading into this opportunity. We'd sold dozens of these testers for $60K to 120K each and were killing it with several mind-blowing over-quota years. Then Gleason surprised us. We were in our old office, an open-concept style former real estate office setup near the Toronto airport. My office was across the front and had big windows looking out onto the busy street along with another glass wall closing off my office from the main office area.

The phone buzzed and the receptionist told me that David Gleason was on the phone for me. The salesman's eye lit up and eyebrows furrowed. What could he possibly want?

"Glenn," Gleason says. "We need 10 of those stingray testers you sell, immediately."

Stingray was the project code name for when the unit was being developed and the name just stuck. I was shocked. I muttered incredulously so my sales guy could catch on.

"You need 10 stingrays delivered right away?" *You've got to be kidding me,* I thought. There was no way he was going to try to pull this a third time.

My salesman breaks the ice for me and asks to put the call on speaker. Stefan is one of the best salespeople I have ever met. A true natural. He started on David with something along the lines of the following.

"Listen, David, we can't waste any more time on your account. Every time we quote you, you just take the quote over to the competition and get a better price. Let's all just save ourselves the trouble. Let's agree we will send you another quote with whatever number you want on it. Of course, again, we both need to agree you can't place an order nor would we accept it with the price, but you can have whatever discount you want. How about 90%? Just remember, David, you *never* buy from us. Soon, we won't be in business, and then the other guys can charge you whatever you want. It's fine to play competitors off against each other, but if in the end, everyone only ever buys from brand A, then brand B will go belly up and you'll be at their mercy. You need to spread it around if you want a healthy market where you can play one off against the other."

David, at this point, is gob smacked. To him, his behavior to date on taking our quotes twice back to the other supplier and using it to get a better price is just standard business practice. It wasn't personal to him, and he was taken aback at how upset Stefan came across.

"No seriously, I need the extra features and measurement accuracy," David countered. "I want to buy your units. I'm willing to order today."

What came out of Stefan's mouth a moment later still rings in my ears to this day. "No, David. No, you don't. You're lying."

"Lying?" David choked on the words.

"Yes, you're a fucking liar and I don't want to play this game anymore."

David himself started to lose composure, but given his background and temperament for negotiation, a swear word here and there doesn't mean much to him.

"Oh really? A liar, eh?" David asks.

"Yes," replies Stefan.

"Ok, answer me this. What's my price verbally on 10 units, delivered quickly, for the top model stingray?"

Stefan wastes no time. "I can get you five percent off, so $95K, and as I like to say, we're open until 5 p.m. and the fax is 1-800-555-1515."

"Ok. Stay on the line," David insists. "Do you hear it ringing?" he says a few moments later. Indeed, the fax ring is heard outside my office. I run to watch what's emerging from the fax. The flow of this paper is so painful with my anticipation. What seems like forever later, I turn over the fax to show a PO for 10 stingray systems. Fully loaded showing a five-percent discount. Total value on the $950K requesting immediate delivery.

"Call me a liar, eh, Stefan? Well, now it's up to you to deliver," Gleason said and hung up. A few weeks later, he called and asked how many more we could deliver in a short period. He wanted another 10 units.

There are times when you need to push back and challenge the customer for their bullshit. Call them a tire kicker, window shopper whatever, by challenging their intent or ability to buy, or perhaps their intention to solicit leverage for them with their desired supplier, puts their integrity on the line.

Beware of the Customer Who Wanted a Ride in a Ferrari

We took on a customer contract with a large global brand name in the telecom industry—a company that caused your ears to perk up and salivation when they called because of the magnitude of business that could follow.

This guy at this giant telecom firm was responsible for bringing watershed deals to our company, and his title might as well have been VP of Huge-Ass Global Partnerships. We were all starstruck and in awe of the company, their people, and the scope of deals they bring. We struck a deal with them and it was *huge*. But the cost was selling your soul to the devil.

I'm ashamed and sheepish to tell this story, but I learned from it and would like to save you the heartache. The executive came to town. Business development true to form, this guy was as big in height and girth as he was in ego and self-importance. He advised us that he refused to stay near our office near the Toronto airport. He only stayed in five-star hotels in major cities. In addition, he informed our VP that he had someone with him (purpose unknown) who would be accompanying him at times. They asked us to make arrangements to take them to a Toronto Maple

Leafs game.

Small trivia fact: Leafs games are *always* sold out. The team had a 13-year sellout streak at one point. People leave the rights to their season tickets in their last will and testament to their heirs, leaving scalping services as the only way to get a ticket to games. We would typically use a ticket service or app to procure seats for key customers, would usually sit in the upper levels—the greens and purples—and everyone was simply happy to be at a Leafs game.

But not this guy. He didn't sit anywhere but platinum. When the VP told me this, I almost shit myself. But what could I do? I ended up buying four tickets since he needed his associate with him and we needed to send our VP, but since we were stuck buying four tickets instead of three, I went as well.

The real rubber hit the road (pun intended) with his next request. The big shot asked our VP to rent him a Ferrari. I shit you not! "Look, when I am in town, you'll treat me like royalty," he said. "I stay in the best hotels (thankfully he paid for his own accommodations), I eat in the best restaurants, and I drive the best cars. I need you guys to get me a car for me to get around in."

Again, what could we do? Tell him no?

Now we spring for both $2,500 Platinum tickets and a three-day Ferrari rental, which costs roughly the same amount per day as a monthly mortgage payment.

We learned our lesson after this extravagant visit. This man was simply abusing naïve partners he sensed he could push around. There was no benefit to us. This guy served no purpose other than setting the stage for the upcoming beatdown we would receive on every scrap of work and supply we were providing. Some might say it was worth it for a huge deal, but you should never be bullied into such lavish spending on a customer whose true value to your company is unknown. If we had been doing business for a year or two and running a win-win deal for everyone (see *everyone's gotta win* for more on this concept), we likely would have been much more inclined to host high-level events. This was not that.

Here are some things I recommend when customers ask you for perks and accommodations:

1. *People are going to ask for free stuff.* The key is how you handle yourself and acting gracefully. Now more than ever, people are looking to get a deal on something. Depending on your business type and the cost of goods or services, these requests can be challenging. Take, for instance, a services business such as equipment maintenance or HVAC service or a software product that does not have an obvious cost. Customers sometimes feel many service, support, or software items should be thrown in for free. You need to develop a firm approach to this mentality.

2. *Always need to remember that it's never about you.* Don't get frazzled, flustered, angry or upset. Take a few breaths and always react calmly and firmly. Working in a small company, one thing I like to do is never position anything in the context of I. The customer may be saying, "Hey, Glenn. I need *you* to give me a discount." My immediate reaction might be to personalize that thinking "you" is me in the singular and I, Glenn, must purvey this imperative discount. At this point I always respond in the collective frame and talk about the company, or we. I also make sure I refer to our offerings in the non-personal. I never say "the value of my services," but rather I say "the company's services."

3. *Shift or move the focus to a discussion on the value of our offering.* I often use the analogy of Mercedes-Benz and say, "Look, if price was the only issue, no one would ever drive a Benz." Customers pick Mercedes for the totality of the value of the brand and work with the dealer on a plan to pay for it. In other words, if I'm looking at a $60,000 luxury car and start talking about paying $45,000, I would likely hear the dealer say perhaps you need to be looking for a C-class instead of an E-class. If you focus on costs alone, you'll

get pulled down into the rabbit hole. The key is to be able to show the value of your products and brand. I have a sales guy, Mike, who has an awesome saying I love. "Look, Mr. Customer. It's a service triangle of good, fast, and cheap. You can pick any two but you can't have all three."

4. *Be firm, but don't embarrass the customer.* Whether they're asking for tickets to a ball game or a Ferrari, even when presents that are "questionable" in terms of ethics or are simply outrageous, you can never, ever embarrass the customer. Remember, you sell your products every day and you've been to the factory and seen the gold fairy dust they sprinkle on the widgets you sell. Don't expect every buyer to have an innate knowledge of your value proposition. If you guffaw at them and state "that's a ridiculous request," you'll embarrass them and the result could be a pull back and diversion over to a vendor who hasn't made them feel stupid. Couch your response with something like, "I understand why you're asking and I respect the position you're in. Let me go over some of what makes up our total cost of ownership."

5. *Focus on the relationship.* We always remind the customer they can post the deal online and get the cheapest price from an unknown vendor or they can work with us. We provide engineers and technologists to ensure you're selecting the right product every time. We offer value pricing in line with all our competitors and you get a dedicated, knowledgeable account manager you can count on for everything. Remind them of past times you saved them from a mistake, or provided flawless service or support (see *Thank God It's Broken*).

6. *Consider loyalty.* If a customer has demonstrated loyalty and in consideration of a longer-term relationship without either party taking the other for granted, it can sometimes be prudent to accommodate partially or even fully on special requests. The key is ensuring you aren't giving away the value for free.

CHAPTER 13

YES MEN GET NO RESPECT

We once had a major supplier we never said no to—until we did. They were a large vendor always in our top five and often number two or three in terms of annual sales. They also had a formidable marketing program with extensive co-op opportunities where they would match our marketing spend dollar for dollar.

In time, we realized the drawbacks of this technique. There may be better ideas for how to spend marketing dollars, but the vendors demand you use up the co-op funds, which requires us to match their desired spend. Us lowering our spend didn't go over well with the supplier. Being they were a billion-dollar company and were used to getting their way, it simply didn't compute for them that we didn't want to increase our appetite for a co-op spend at the same rate as they did. The way this manifested was equally frustrating and telling about how outside influences can attempt to manipulate a company. First, they approached their primary marketing contact, then they approached his boss, and then me.

Our answers were all uniform and consistent. After hearing no from the entire marketing team, they took to bringing up the matter in a sales meeting that included the North American sales manager and the president of the company. They painted a picture for the bigwigs. "Your idiots in marketing are passing an offer of $70K to 100K in extra funds without giving it a second thought."

The president and sales manager looked at me as if I had just flushed $70,000 down the toilet without even speaking to them. I took a simple and direct approach.

"Ok, fine. There are three of us in the room. I've already voted, and frankly, it's my decision, and the answer is no. If you can convince these two why we should spend that money, hire an extra person to deploy these funds, and make all these extra commitments, they can outvote me." Then I turned to my two coworkers and said, "Don't forget the quota and objectives you both signed off on for our division." Devoting the extra resources simply wasn't in our plans.

My decision prevailed, but for the duration of our relationship it remained strained. Ultimately, we moved on from this relationship but the lesson I learned can boiled down to *don't let the tail wag the dog.*

The second issue that arose at the same time we turned down the extra funding was centered around *what* the big supplier wanted us to advertise. They'd switched from a co-op manner of supporting our marketing efforts to trying to control the content, tone, strategy, and message of our content. They began to attempt to change our corporate culture and messaging in opposition to our values and beliefs. Specifically, they were arguing we should switch to a method which would cast our competitors in a negative light and was tantamount to competitor bashing.

We prided ourselves on maintaining professional relations with all our competitors.

Even when the supplier realized we wouldn't spend the extra money, they continued to try and manipulate the corporate value message we portrayed in our ads. I'm proud to say we never wavered once and told them to pound salt. This also fed into our decision to move on to another partnership.

The stressful part was the constant barrage at all levels of staff about how great this idea was. They took different key staff members out to lunch, attempting to manipulate them into seeing how we were missing excellent opportunities to send a message to the target audience. I would then have to fend off these backhanded inquiries from staff and executives about this *unique opportunity* the supplier was presenting us for marketing. It was tedious and shady.

The lesson I learned was that money, be it contributions, donations, co-ops, or loans, comes with strings attached. People wish to control the manner in which the funds are provided, how they're received, and how they're deployed. Before accepting these kinds of funds from suppliers and external stakeholders, ensure you have the right safeguards and structures in place to remain in control of the contribution so that they're not used as a tool to manipulate you. Say no when you don't agree. Say yes when you do, and never fall into a habit of always saying yes or no, because if you do, it'll become the expectation that inevitably leads to resentment when you decide to one day break the pattern.

Implied Familiarity Also Breeds Contempt

Have you ever heard that saying, "familiarity breeds contempt?" The definition of it is extensive knowledge of or close association with someone or something leads to a loss of respect for them or it. While the concept is ancient, the phrase is credited to English writer Geoffrey Chaucer, who used those words in his work *Tale of Melibee* in the 1300s.[19]

The phrase is another way of saying as time goes on, people have more time to learn things they dislike about you, other people, or things. The point is not to debate the causes, effects, or ways and means of avoiding becoming contemptuous towards others that you grow close to.

There's one key takeaway to this concept. Before you engage in any action, ask yourself, "Will this behavior or idiosyncrasy increase or decrease

---

19 "Familiarity breed contempt," Grammarist, accessed September 13, 2021, https://grammarist.com/proverb/familiarity-breeds-contempt/.

attraction or increase contempt in the people around me?"

Let's use a simple example. You go to your brother and sister-in-law's for dinner every few weeks. When you finish dinner do you:

A.   Leave your plate on the table and let someone else clean up after you?

B.   Put your plate in the sink?

C.   Rinse your plate and put it in the dishwasher?

Notice the power of three coming out in this example? It goes without saying with only those three choices available to you, choice C is most likely to not cause an increase in contempt. Can you imagine Sally saying to your brother, "For God's sakes, Brian, your brother never picks up after himself. He either leaves the table and leaves it for us or   throws   his plate in the sink like we're running a cafeteria. Why can't he put his shit in the dishwasher like the rest of us?"

When I interact with people, I always think through situations and ask myself questions about how my behaviors will be received—particularly when I'm in someone else's home or business.

And finally, the true essence of this lesson is a take on this age-old saying familiarity breeds contempt, and that's *implied familiarity also breeds contempt*. Have you ever had a customer act overly personal with you? Perhaps he was stalking you on Facebook or Instagram and making assumptions about your preferences?

For instance, he stumbled across a bunch of photos with you fishing and in a boat. He starts off on some bogus tirade about his fishing exploits and how avid he is at bass or trout fishing. You start wondering where the this coming from, and then he lets it slip that he found you on Instagram and saw you on a boat holding a trout.

"Oh yeah, that's my father-in-law's boat," you say. "To be honest, Jack, I fucking hate fishing. I only go because my wife makes me. They all force me to love it because her dad does and it keeps the peace. But honestly, I dread those early mornings freezing my butt off. I'd much prefer relaxing on the porch with a hot coffee and catching up on my reading."

"Oh," he says. "My bad."

People feign this familiarity all the time, and I find it highly annoying. I would prefer people to take the time and apply other skills discussed in this book to actually get to know me and my preferences. I can assure you, if you feign familiarity it will create contempt in others, so don't do it.

Always Check Emails

There are so many ways for us to communicate. Phone calls, video conferences, social media, text messages, and encrypted apps. But now, more than ever, emails have taken over our communication. And yet, many people send emails incorrectly.

One of my biggest pet peeves is that email is often treated the same as text messages, full of garbled text and lacking salutations or a closing signature. People often open emails without using the person's name and send short, incomplete messages. Maybe I'm a stickler, but from my old school mentality, it isn't acceptable to skip basic email etiquette while multitasking because it comes at the cost of professionalism. For me, the right email messaging represents the difference between an opportunity and getting deleted, between starting a dialogue and getting screened.

Here are the rules I follow for professional emails:

Proofread, Spell and Grammar Check

Use email programs with robust spell checkers, and if needed, buy yourself a subscription to Grammarly or a similar digital writing assistance tool. Proofread your important emails before sending. Read it again and read it aloud. Show it to someone else nearby to see if your message is clear. Make sure your tone is appropriate and that your email doesn't come across as sloppy. Far too often, someone will tap out an email on their phone or use a speak-to-text tool to dictate their messages, and the final result will be an illegible mess.

Check and Prioritize the Addressee(s)

When I'm writing important emails, I always leave the email addresses off the "To" and "Cc" lines. This way, it's impossible to accidentally send an email before it is ready to go. If you do accidentally click "send," it will prompt you to "enter addresses."

Once the proofreading is done and you're satisfied with the message content, it's time to consider the addressee. You need to consider the use of "To" versus "Cc," or "carbon copy." Have you ever received an email with an unclear action because everyone's address is in the "To" field?

This is how we designate things at my firm:

The "To" field is for those requested or expected to act (could be multiple people). If the email does not require someone's direct attention, do not put them in the "To" line. The "Cc" field is simply for their information with no expectation that they will take action on the email, other than receive it.

Once you have now proofread your email and added the appropriate "To" and "Cc" people and are satisfied everything is good, check again that you are sending it to the right person. Is it the correct Marc or is it Mark? Did you spell the recipient's name correctly in the salutation? We have a lot of Marcs in our company, and it's poor form to start the email with "Hi Mark."

The Subject Line Matters. Make Them Count

The subject line should summarize what your email is about. It should be short, sweet, and to the point. If I can tell the whole story in three- to five-word titles that are concise, then I do just that. Save the reader time and allow them the opportunity to scan subject lines and determine if the email is something they can open later or if it's something they need to respond to immediately. Make sure you clearly state what your email is about without the recipient needing to open it. Use the wrong subject line, and the recipient is liable to ignore it and let it pile up in their inbox, never to be opened.

Listen to Grandma and Mind Your Manners

Just like your grandparents and parents taught you as a kid, mind your

Ps and Qs and learn early that please and thank you could represent the razor's edge between getting a response and getting ignored. Ask politely when posing questions, and when someone responds with answers to questions or sends you a document you requested, follow up with a quick thanks. Manners matter, and more importantly, they show you're a professional and a nice person. They also show respect for the other person.

It's Not a Novel, So Don't Write a Book

This ranks up there near the top of my pet peeves. If you find you need to write paragraph upon paragraph to explain yourself, you probably need to consider picking up the phone rather than sending an email. Many times people feel that they can't avoid sending a lengthy email with important information or detailed instructions. However, more often than not, those long emails cause confusion and frustration and really only result in more emails asking for more explanations. For this reason, it's important to keep your emails concise and decide before you send if it's the best method of communication.

Check Your Attachments

This is one of my golden rules at my firm. When anyone starts with us and spends any time with me, I hammer this rule into your psyche. First, check that all relevant documents are attached. Then the last thing you do before hitting send is open every attachment, scan them quickly, and verify they're the correct documents. For instance, it's important to check the changes were saved and showing, and then complete a final check to ensure you're not sending the wrong document. I learned this the hard way years ago when I sent the wrong people the wrong documents that I did not want them to see. You cannot unsend these once the customer has seen them. Don't ever skip this rule.

Your Email Signature Should Be Perfect

All email programs allow for multiple signatures. My attitude is brief informative email signatures are best as long as all relevant information is needed for the person you're replying to. At a bare minimum, make sure your phone number is on *every* signature version. How many times have you searched for someone's name in your email so you can phone them, and there are 40 emails from this person and literally none of them have a proper signature with full contact details? Seriously, when this happens to me, I feel like it's a firing offense. I always send them an email and write, "Hey, what's your phone number? I checked all of your emails and none of them have proper contact details." Hopefully, they can read between the lines how frustrating this is. Your standard signature should typically include your name, job title, company name, email address, and website, LinkedIn URL, and phone number where you can be reached. You may also want to include a company banner on initial emails with company highlights. Remember to ensure your email has a responsive design and that it will look good on mobile devices. Here are the versions I use depending on the recipient:

Example Full Signature, with Title

Best Regards,

Glenn Poulos

Vice President & General Manager

AcmeTech Solutions Inc

2880 Any Road, Anywhere, ON L5N 7X8

p: (905) 555-1211

m: (416) 555-1313

f: (905) 555-1414

e: glenn.poulos@acmetech.com

www.acmetech.com

Example Full Signature, Without Title

Best Regards,

Glenn Poulos

AcmeTech Solutions Inc

2880 Any Road, Anywhere, ON L5N 7X8

p: (905) 555-1211

m: (416) 555-1313
f: (905) 555-1414
e: glenn.poulos@acmetech.com
www.acmetech.com

Example Reply with No Details

Best Regards,
Glenn
p: (905) 555-1211

When your message is ready and you've addressed all of these areas, then—and only then—should you hit send.

Respond to All Emails

When someone emails you, do your best to reply within 24 hours. If I need more time to reply, I typically ask for it.

If receiving unsolicited emails (see the chapter Implied Familiarity also Breeds Contempt), I don't feel the need to reply. Given my position in the company, I receive so much email I have to prioritize what emails make it to the read-worthy stage. We have a team email system, and I can easily move messages from salespeople for services that apply to other departments like logistics, accounting, and payroll, and they can decide how to respond. If the message is not on point or irrelevant I delete it and do not reply.

Follow the tips above, and do everything you can to avoid getting deleted.

CHAPTER 14

CHECKING AND LEAVING VOICEMAILS—MY HARSHEST LESSON

You're probably rolling your eyes at this chapter topic. *Everyone knows how to check and leave a voicemail message, for God's sake.*

But this chapter contains one of the harshest lessons I've ever learned—a moment that's burned into my psyche and represents a source of unmitigated embarrassment for me. Like so many other tough lessons in life, once you rip the band-aid off your bruised ego, you find yourself telling this story to everyone you come across when offering coaching advice. My story comes from 2006, when I was serving as the president of the wireless division of the company I founded in 1991.

I was also going through a divorce and settling into a routine as a newly single part-time parent (Wednesdays and every other weekend). This time was a rough patch for me. I was feeling broken and battered. Those aren't excuses—I'm simply explaining the context before getting to the story.

One day, I was engaged in conversation with one of our salespeople, Bob, about a topic and he was asking for my help. This typically consisted of joining calls for important customer meetings and assisting in getting the right product package and pricing for big deals. At one point in the conversation, the sales guy explained what he was going to need.

"No problem," I told him. "If you need something, just give me a call. If I am not there, leave me a voicemail." The salesman started laughing, the type of laugh that bursts through pursed lips with a choke in their throat and a huff from their nose, where one would be soaked with liquid had the person been taking a sip from a drink. "What's so funny?" I asked, perplexed.

"You're kidding, right?" he responded.

"No, why would I be kidding?"

"Call you and leave a voicemail?" he asked.

I retorted promptly. "Yes, for Christ's sake, call me and leave me a voicemail and I'll get back to you."

"I guess you haven't heard the standing joke then?"

By this point, I was flustered and frustrated, along with a host of other emotions. "No, Bob, I haven't heard the joke. Why don't you enlighten me?"

"Hey, don't shoot the messenger," he warned. "I will tell you, but I'm just passing it on. I didn't make it up."

"Ok. So what is it?"

"Well, there's a standard joke in the company about contacting you. People say, 'Oh, give him a call and leave him a voicemail,' and everyone laughs, because it's an inside joke. The reality, Glenn, is that *everyone* knows that you *never* answer their calls, and when we leave a voicemail, you never listen to them. And even if you did, you never call us back. The running joke is now trimmed down to the shortened version, 'Oh just leave him a voicemail,' laugh laugh, giggle giggle.

"Glenn," the salesman continued, "The only way to speak to you is to speak to you. You are famous for being the most completely unavailable person on the phone and for never returning a call. Other forms of the joke are, 'Oh, just give him a call,' or 'he'll call you back.'"

At this point, the world was spinning and I was almost in tears. I choke up easy hearing stories and telling stories. I needed to extract myself from this situation and deal with what I had just been told. *Could this be true?* In my heart of hearts, I knew it was. An even harsher lesson was staring me down the face in the coming months as our company's corporate owner forced us into bankruptcy, and myself and 100 other employees all lost our jobs.

I made many promises when I started my next job, but I made sure that responding to calls and voicemails was a core tenet of my business behavior. Now, if you call me, I will answer the phone unless I am indisposed. If you leave a message or not, I will call you back. The only exception to this rule is obvious spam calls. Most of the time, I even return voicemails from random salespeople, as long as they have a reasonable justification for calling me.

I've acted on this rule for the past 14 years. I'm so reliable, in fact, that on our switchboard system, I'm the final failover for all inbound calls. If you don't make it to the correct department or end up in an automated attendant loop, I'm the last ring you will get. Thus, if your inbound call comes to me you get to speak to the owner. If you leave me a voicemail, you'll get a call back. If a customer calls looking for an invoice, I will assign the message to an accounting member and set a boomerang reminder to ensure they do it.

I've seen reflections of my past behavior in many people over the years. I don't approach them directly and say, "Hey, don't be a loser and call people back!" I simply find the appropriate moment and ask if they want to hear about my most embarrassing moment in business.

Make Your Voicemails Count

Leaving compelling voicemails require its own set of rules—and not in a mode of VMLMCB (voicemail, left message to call me back), which is one of the most annoying crutches I hear from salespeople and is highlighted elsewhere. There are times, however, when VMLMCB is your only option.

I like to coach my team with the following rules when leaving voicemails. I have adopted these rules when I'm on the one doing the calling:

1. Keep it short and sweet, 30 seconds max.

2. Don't call and hang up without leaving a message. If you call them, leave a voicemail.

3. Use your normal tone of voice. No need for elevated moods or radio voice-overs. Speak at a normal speed and don't sound desperate.

4. After you hear the beep, start your message with a brief greeting and offer relevant information.

5. Ask a question you wouldn't pose in an email, or if the issue is sensitive, suggest that you had something to ask them.

6. Don't use a traditional close.

7. Leave voicemails at the beginning or end of the day.

8. Always leave your phone number. Don't say "You've got my number."

Keep It Short and Sweet

The ideal length of a voicemail is an age-old rule that I didn't make up and is great advice to abide by. Have you glanced at your phone and seen there's a voicemail from an unknown number and it's only a few seconds long? I have, and I normally delete them. Real people, especially business contacts, generally don't leave six-second voicemails.

On the other hand, if I start listening to a voicemail and realize it's two minutes long, there's almost no chance I will listen to the whole thing. I will likely say to myself, "Hey Bob, ramble much? Get to the point," as I delete the message and make a mental note to call Bob back.

A succinct, 30-second message is the sweet spot. It gives you time to spark curiosity without the customer needing to find a relaxing place to listen to your voicemail story.

If You Call, Leave a Voicemail

If you're going to take the time to call a prospect, you have to leave a message. Otherwise, you're liable to lower your standing in the customer's eyes. The customer is probably screening their calls and may not have time to speak with you right now, but don't let them think your call must not be important, or worse, that you're a scam call.

If you call a few times without leaving messages, you will have essentially screened yourself out—and if you dial the guy five times a day and drown his phone in voicemails, he's liable to take out an electronic restraining order on you and block your number. Which is why balance is key. Call, leave a voicemail, and wait three days or a week, whatever is suitable. A professional message to an appropriate target will draw a feeling of reciprocity to call you back and give you an answer.

Use Your Normal Tone of Voice

Remember, you're not a morning show host on 103.3 HITZ FM and weren't recruited as a high school pep rally announcer. There's nothing worse than grinding through a busy day checking voicemails and stumbling across a burst of fake excitement. "Hey, Glenn. It's Bob Johnson from ACME Marketing. How are you doing on this beautiful day? I'm unbelievably fantastic. In fact, you could say I'm feeling amazing. Have I got an offer for you that you don't want to miss." Delete. I can hear him leaving this same message to 100 other clients. If it sounds like someone is dialing for dollars and getting their 20, 50, or 100 prospecting calls done for the day, many customers will feel completely absolved from having to respond. Use a normal tone of voice and be yourself.

Start Your Message With a Brief Greeting

Once the tone of voice is set, you want to open the message with a greeting and offer relevant information. Be careful about sounding like the standard sales rep. For instance, don't start with, "Hi Bob, my name is Sam Spade and I work for ACME Marketing." Instead, start with a question they don't usually hear on voicemails. Here's an arbitrary example. "Hey Bob, it's Sam from ACME Robotics. Have you folks started deploying AI in your factory floor robotics?" If you can make it personal and specific, they're more likely to be intrigued to respond.

Obviously, you need to have a close on your voicemail, and this is where

I warn salespeople to skip the traditional, "Please call me back," or "I'll circle back in a few days." Instead offer something compelling. "We would like to show your team how other clients have achieved 40% to 60% speed enhancement with these AI upgrades and how they increase ROI in less than a year." Finish with your name and contact info. "Again, it's Glenn Poulos with ACME Robotics at 416-555-1212. Thanks for your time."

Leave Voicemails at the Beginning or End of the Day

A nugget I gleaned a long time ago is to leave voicemails at the end of the day. Why is this? It has to do with how people process information and what's known as the serial position effect. This psychological phenomenon says when you show people a list, they'll remember the first and last items the best. So once again, if you can't be first you want to be the last thing they hear.

Always Leave Your Phone Number

The recipient is listening to your message, so don't make them do extra work. If you fail to leave your phone number, it's far less likely that you'll get a callback. You never want someone to have to dig around or check their call records in hopes of tracking down your number. Make it as easy as possible for someone to reach you.

Example Script

"Hey Bob, it's Glenn Poulos from ACME Robotics. I was wondering: have you folks started deploying AI in your factory floor robotics? We would like to show your team how other clients have achieved 40% to 60% speed enhancement with these AI upgrades and how they ROI in less than a year I'll follow up with an email, but I'd love to continue this conversation. Once again, it's Glenn Poulos with ACME Robotics at 416-555-1212. Thanks for your time."

Orders Solve a Lot of Problems

To coin a phrase most often attributed to Google Executive Chairman Eric Schmidt, "Revenue solves all problems."[20] The quote reminds me of a saying I've been using for years: "Listen Jack, orders solve a lot of problems."

We learned this lesson in the toughest of ways during one of our expansion phases into the United States. We'd decided to branch out beyond our standard territory with one of our business groups and began the process of hiring people (the wrong ones, as it turned out) all across the core territories in the U.S. We had a top-notch sales manager who was an incredible salesperson. Years later, in fact, he hung up his manager badge and returned to direct sales, and I heard him say a couple years later that he was never happier. He was now working normal hours with almost no travel and a predictable income.

He flew around the U.S. scouring areas for direct salespeople for us to hire and employ. Of course, in addition to hiring the staff, and seeing we were in Canada, we needed to establish mechanisms for U.S. payroll, medical benefits, and all the various tax and government remittances required for making payroll in another country.

After a few months, we had accumulated staff in what we considered the key areas of Northern and Southern California, Florida, Texas, upstate New York, and Seattle and had six staff working for us full time. I was amazed at the pace we accumulated staff and was proud when I spoke of our organization and how it had grown. I considered us unstoppable, and it was a great feeling.

After six to nine months, once the start-up phase language like "he's just getting going," and "she's just establishing herself," had worn off, we began to notice something troubling.

There were almost no orders.

---

20 Derek Thompson, "'Schmidt: 'Revenue Solves All Problems,' in Business and Government," *The Atlantic*, October 5, 2011, https://www.theatlantic.com/business/archive/2011/10/schmidt-revenue-solves-all-problems-in-business-and-government/246209/.

Here and there, we would encounter an odd lucky break and get a nice pop that was just enough to keep us going. "We just need to give it some more time," we kept saying. We spent tens of thousands on travel, sending our best managers and staff down to the states to help our new staff prospect, and were convinced success was just around the corner.

As time went on, we started to notice some other things. The manager showed up in Texas one day for a sales call and after renting a car, he headed over to our sales rep's home office, only to find him still in pajamas at 10 a.m. and having totally forgot he was coming. On another visit to Seattle, he was stunned to find out that the rep—knowing the manager was coming for several weeks—had not booked any calls. He was convinced that our brand should sell ourselves and his reputation should be enough to gather orders, yet to date those orders had all but eluded him.

We ultimately realized there was a combination of problems. First, we'd hired seasoned reps who managed active territories where there were well-defined customers and were used to the phones ringing. There were also a few hires where we cut corners and hired people who were less than cut out for sales. In truth, the company was not completely free of blame and culpability. We'd made a strategic miscalculation and broke one of my cardinal rules without even realizing it.

We had no business hiring people and expecting people would buy from us. There was no compelling reason for customers to change. And, unlike in Canada, there were at least five other well-established competitors in the United States that had decades of proven reputation. All we really had was a desire that they buy from us, and although I clearly point out in a previous chapter that number three and four aren't worth it, we were actually number five or worse in some cases.

This foray taught us one final lesson. We were making tons of money in several of our Canadian business units and the profits were significant, to the point that they masked the mistakes we were making. Instead of Eric Schmidt's idea that "revenue solves all problems," we were showcasing how "revenue masks many problems." We were not blind to the poor results, but we were basically numb to the bad performance because the other divisions were propping it up and allowing us to be far more forgiving than we should have been.

Over time, we began to adjust the specific salespeople, as we couldn't tolerate people selling in their pajamas or allow others to continue who felt sales calls were beneath them. Unfortunately, the worst possible storm occurred, and when profitability slipped in Canada, we could no longer kid ourselves. There was a stark realization that our core was in jeopardy, and I was faced with making a tough decision.

During difficult times, I always remember what I heard General Norman Schwarzkopf say during Desert Shield when asked about leading over 100,000 men across a desert and into what would likely be a life changing battle. "When placed in command, take charge," he said. One of the most important jobs of a leader is not to do the most work or be the best at everything. Rather, their key function is to make decisions and take charge. On that fateful day in October that we refer to as Black Monday, I decided to close the U.S. operation and let the direct sales force go.

In the end, the U.S. operation could have thrived, and almost any other problem was solvable with a few orders and some profits. Conversely, don't let profitable business mask problems in other areas. If there are no orders, there is no business.

CHAPTER 15

CABLES AND CONNECTORS

In our business, we sell electronic equipment and systems. These items are connected together with cables, connectors, adapters, and various other components. An example setup is below:

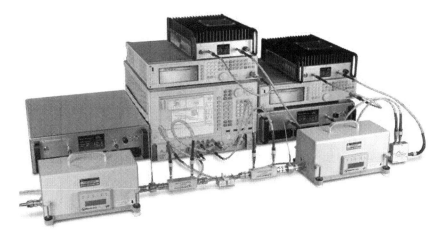

We make most of our money selling instruments like these. Many customers only buy these once every few years. However, they buy cables and connection devices throughout the year. By ensuring you're the dominant supplier for these base business supplies, you can learn when things are evolving. Be sure to ask about equipment needs every time they buy or make an inquiry on miscellaneous items.

When they ask for a quote on cables, I'm sure to *never fax the facts* (the quote) or *ship the shit* (samples), and I'm sure to *have something in my hand* (donuts, promo items, literature, etc.) and *something in my mind* (ideas for better cables or setup methods) when I show up to deliver the quote they asked for.

Intermittent Reinforcement

Intermittent reinforcement is a conditioning schedule in which a reward or punishment (reinforcement) is not administered every time the desired response is performed. Instead of the mouse receiving cheese every time it pushes the button, it might only receive the reward every few times. This makes receiving the reward random and unpredictable.

Gambling is also an example of intermittent reinforcement. If you only won or only lost every time you spun the wheel on a slot machine, it would no longer be exciting or fun. Intermittent rewards are necessary or the players will stop playing. When the reinforcement is intermittent, it causes a euphoric response in the brain (joy feeling).

There are four basic types of intermittent schedules of reinforcement:

1. Fixed-ratio (FR) schedule.

2. Variable-ratio (VR) schedule.

3. Fixed-interval (FI) schedule.

4. Variable-interval (VI) schedule.

Fixed-ratio schedules are those in which the response is reinforced only after a specific number of responses. An example of a fixed-ratio schedule would be getting your coffee or sandwich card punched at your favorite fast-food place, and after 10 punches on the card, you receive a free coffee or sandwich. This schedule produces a steady rate of responding with typically only brief pauses between. In simple terms, people tend to repeat the behavior consistently while they're working toward the 10 punches on their card. Once the reward has been received, however, they may pause in the desired behavior before beginning again. They might get sick of that brand of sandwich or coffee and switch to something else. Fixed-ratio schedules don't guarantee continuous behavior after the reward is given.

Variable-ratio (VR) schedules occur when a response is reinforced after an unpredictable number of responses. This has proven to create a steady and high rate of responding. The perfect example of variable-ratio schedules are lottery games or gambling. Under lab testing conditions with animals such as rats, a good example would be providing food pellets after three taps on a button and then again after one, then after five, and on and on. This might seem confusing at first, but ultimately this method is very effective at garnering repetitive behaviors. The key aspect of variable-ratio schedule is the reinforcement schedule in which the reward is given occurs only after an unpredictable number of responses. Panjo's Pizza, my local pizza delivery place around the corner, uses a VR approach. Every once in a while, and I never know when, the driver hands me a $25 gift certificate to use on future purchases. He offers me a sincere thank you for my business and acknowledges me verbally that I'm a great customer. Although the schedule is variable, there's a pattern and a reward that's given.

Fixed-interval schedules are those where the response or reward is given after a specific amount of time, be it every 30 seconds, every month, or every year. This effect typically causes high amounts of the desired behavior to occur near the end of the interval but the behavior typically slows down immediately after the reward is given. An example of a fixed-interval schedule would be giving students a quiz every Monday. You can rest assured that on the weekend students will be studying feverishly. Once the quiz is taken on Monday, the students are rewarded with their grade and recognition. Studying for that subject typically drops to lowest level for the week. In short, fixed-interval reinforcement results in a fairly significant drop-off in desired behaviors post reward and the desired behavior tends to increase gradually as the time to the next reward draws closer.

Variable-interval schedules occur when a response is rewarded after an unpredictable amount of time has passed, and this has shown to produce a steady rate of response. A classic example of variable-interval reinforcement is a pop quiz. Students know pop quizzes will occur, but teachers never tell the students when they will happen. This causes students to be alert at all times during class and study throughout the subject periods. If the student exhibits good behavior, they'll know the subject matter and will likely get an A or relatively good mark on the quiz, which is their reward. Another perfect example of this is the pesky speed trap on your main route to work. It's in place sometimes but not always—and the knowledge of the speed trap being in place causes you to adopt the approach of never speeding on that throughfare. The reward of never getting a ticket.

Summary of Reinforcement Examples

Reinforcement Schedule	Description	Result
Fixed Ratio (FR)	Reinforcement is delivered after a predictable number of responses (e.g., after 10, 20, 30, and 40 responses).	High response rate. Pauses occur after reinforcement.
Variable Ratio (VR)	Reinforcement is delivered after an unpredictable number of responses (e.g., after 1, 6, 4, and 7 responses).	High and steady response rate.

Reinforcement Schedule	Description	Result
Fixed Interval (FI)	Reinforcement is delivered at predictable time intervals (e.g., after 10 minutes, or 30 days, etc.).	Moderate response rate. Significant pauses after reinforcement.
Variable Interval (VI)	Reinforcement is delivered at unpredictable time intervals (e.g., after seven, three, nine, and four minutes).	Moderate yet steady response rate.

Using an Appropriate Schedule Requires Analysis

When you're trying to teach a new behavior, a continuous schedule is often the best choice. However, once the behavior is learned you might need to change to a variable schedule. Typically in business, variable schedules occur more often than fixed schedules. For instance, if you offered a customer a free item every time they placed an order, over time, instead of the gift being seen as a positive reinforcement, it would become expected. If not presented every time, the lack of reward could be seen as negative reinforcement.

Freebies and incentives should only be given on a highly unpredictable reinforcement schedule. The intermittent aspect of this will produce a higher likelihood of repeated behavior. Repeat buyers will come to appreciate intermittent rewards or incentives such as meals and entertainment.

If a reward is given too often and repeatably, it can become undesired. Imagine every time you visit a customer they expect to take them out to lunch. It could lead the customer to stop dealing with you because they've been overindulged and the reward is no longer wanted.

Don't get me wrong, it's great to reward customers, and there are myriad ways to accomplish this. Just be wary about overdoing it. Be generous but don't always buy lunch for your customer, and if they offer to buy you lunch randomly, be gracious and accept. If you're taking them out to lunch, vary the venue between the Ruth's Chris and In-N-Out Burger. Sometimes make it expensive and sometimes go on the cheap. Be sure to keep it completely random. When you reward the customer every time in the same way, they don't appreciate it and will often will hold you in contempt.

Ambivalent Line Loss Factor

The first company that I started was in October of 1991. The six years prior to that, I worked at my first sales job. This is the same job where all of the owners had matching BMW 7 series cars.

During this time, I joined forces with a coworker and a buddy in a similar business and struck out on our own. My goal was to start my first business by 30, and I made it with a cool six months to spare. Our business model centered around approaching companies from around the world. It might be a tech company in Australia, Spain, or the U.S., and we'd serve as their sales force in Canada, similar to what reps do in the United States, where they'd sell for a company then get a commission. We served the same kind of function, but in Canada, we operated as a distributor, buying goods from these companies and importing them into Canada.

Back in '91, we started the company with one very small line (a "line" is a vendor). There was a trade show in Florida that October called the RF Expo. Myself and the two guys who started the company hopped on a plane and flew down to Florida. I rented out a single room for the three of us, and the cheapest car. But when I went to pick up the car, I had a change of heart. "We've gotta show up in style," I thought, so I upgraded to a Cadillac. When we piled into this Caddy to go to the show, we felt like a million bucks. We were entrepreneurs, striking out on our own, and it's tough to describe how special that moment felt. There was a lot of fear of the unknown obviously, but there was also exhilaration.

We would go to these shows and approach companies and say, "What are you doing for sales in Canada?" Some already had a rep. Others were looking for one.

We went around looking for vendors. We thought we could sell to our existing customers that weren't covered in Canada and sign them up. Back then, because we were so light on product and revenue, our standards were pretty low. Did they breathe? Did the products function? Were the lights on in the building? Ok, sign 'em up! That became the modus operandi. With our latest company now approaching its 15th anniversary, when a good 'line' comes along we sit down and discuss it. When we all agree the response is still the exact same as it was 30 years ago—sign 'em up!

It took time to realize that pursuing number three and four lines doesn't make any sense. I learned those rules the hard way. We'd sign up the number four line, and then we'd bring it to our customers, and they'd say no. When we signed up these lines, we realized that there were other companies that had done what we did before.

At the time, I was 29 and still wasn't super savvy to all of our competitors. There were two or three companies that really had done an amazing job of building a product portfolio where they had 20 or 30 vendors, but six or seven were number ones. Another company had 20 lines with four or five number ones.

I quickly started to realize all the number ones were taken, and so were the number twos! In fact, there was so much competition that you really had to struggle in order to build a valid product portfolio, which in our in lingo is called a *line card*.

We did what we could, and sometimes we got lucky. We had a good solid line in the number one-two range and had a little niche. In essence, they'd actually created the catalyst opportunity for us to start the company. And then we got another line that was dissatisfied with their sales force in Canada. They knew us from before, and they wanted to work with us. This ended up being what really put us on the map.

Soon we came to realize with so many one and two brands accounted for, and the only way we were going to build our portfolio, would be to steal brands. This is when a whole new set of lessons came into play began.

I had to be bold, embrace fear and greed, and call these companies that were already represented.

The one guy who had a little bevy of product lines that we liked was named David Gleason. Yes, he is the same David Gleason who later started a manufacturer we referenced earlier in the book. He was our competitor and had some really, really good lines, so I called and asked if his customers were satisfied working with him and if there was any room for change.

I would then pattern a follow-up system to reconnect with them religiously over time. Lo and behold, one day I managed to get one of them to say yes. Wow, I did it! I scraped away one of his lines and felt like a genius. Gleason was one guy who was actually a little shorter than me. But he had a huge personality and commanded a lot of authority. He had a lot of business and a lot of big customers under his control, and even though he was twice my age, I basically feared him.

When the next trade show came, I see David walking toward me as soon as I turn down an aisle. Dammit, I thought, he's going to kill me for stealing his line away. Since I didn't want there to be bad blood, I greeted him and mumbled an apology about stealing away his product line.

"You have to realize something about me," he said, and this is where the golden rule was delivered. "There's never been a line that I've ever had that left me that I wanted to keep." Christ, I thought. I just took a line that he didn't care about anymore. My gain was his ambivalent line loss. Factor! Ultimately, we came to learn this line was passe and the sales were nominal at best.

When the customer or vendor is important to you, you need to treat them like they're your most important asset. You can't ignore your number one. The same applies to your lines in your sales business.

Never Get a Black Couch

I learned this lesson at my 15-year-old company that went under right after we were acquired by a public company. I've carried the lesson I learned from this forward. In that company, my brother was president of one of the divisions, and I was president of one of the other divisions. It was quite a large executive office, and we shared it. We ended up buying one of those partners desks, consisting of two desks that are initially constructed as one larger desk, and you sit on either side of it, facing each other.

The desks were located in the middle of the room, and we had two leather chairs and a comfortable black couch. The whole idea behind the black couch was that if someone came into your office and wanted to talk to you, they inevitably would end up sitting on the black couch. By virtue of it being there, we created an environment for someone to sit down and comfortably relax.

The black couch also came with unseen and misunderstood expectations. When people came in and sat down, we were showing them that we had this unlimited source of money—after all, we could afford this awesome black couch. We had this business with multiple divisions and were part of a public company. They saw the couch and thought money.

People would sit on this black couch and tell us about their great business opportunities. They had everything they needed, except for one thing: money. The idea could have been good, bad, or indifferent, but they were always looking for the same thing. You have to realize the subtlety I am building up to, and that it's that they never came looking for management assistance. They never needed warehouse space or to leverage our sales teams to promote their great idea. There was only one thing they ever wanted whilst sitting on the proverbial black couch. Money!

CHAPTER 16

MARCONI PIZZA FACTOR

One day at work, I was starving, so I decided to order myself a pizza from Marconi, my favorite pizza joint. When I say favorite it barely does it justice. If this was my last day on earth and I had to order my last supper, there's no question it would be Marconi's.

This was in the late 1990s, and there were about 15 people who worked in the office. I thought it would be selfish to order only for myself, and if I ordered one pie, it wouldn't be enough to feed everyone who might want a slice. I was in a good mood, and it was a Friday, so I decided to order enough pizza for everybody.

"Lunch is on me," I told everyone.

The next week, I thought, that was so fun ordering pizza for everyone, I'm going to do it again. So, I did. Soon enough, pizza became a weekly thing for the office. I would place an order for Marconi, and everyone would enjoy a slice or two. This Friday pizza tradition went on for a while. But on one particular Friday, I had to respond to a customer and drop something off, so I turned to Sally, one of my co-workers, to handle the task.

"Can you order lunch for everybody? I'll be back at noon sharp,"

I told her.

As you can imagine, after meeting with the customer, I was hungry and excited to get back to the office and eat my favorite meal. I made a beeline to the boardroom where we normally put the pizza. But something wasn't right. I couldn't smell my favorite pizza in the air.

When I looked at the table, I found Chinese food.

What the fuck is this?!

I asked Sally about the Chinese food immediately, because I *hate* Chinese fast food.

"We're sick of pizza," she told me.

After that, it became a weekly debate. "Well, we can't have pizza this week, we just had it last week." From that point, I was still on the hook for buying lunch for everyone every Friday for a half-dozen years, and was still buying lunch for everybody until the day the company was closed down by our corporate parent. We never canceled our Friday lunches, even when we hit hard times.

In the end, we had 50 people in the office, and two or three staff members were derailed all Friday morning preparing the lunch, because they would have to go to the grocery store and get fresh chicken and salad, because it had to be healthy and we couldn't always have pizza, and so sometimes we ordered shawarma. A guy in the warehouse would even drive his pickup to Costco to get different flavors of pop. Instead of Coke or Pepsi, we were pandering to everything. Some people only like Crush, and others wanted Ginger Ale. But then others spoke up and wanted diet Ginger Ale, and someone else wanted soda water.

I made a point in my current company to never make the same mistake again. I stuck to that promise through the first 14 years of running my current business. But then, the COVID-19 pandemic happened. We had a skeleton crew in the office, and I decided to get pizza for the team on Fridays, a little pick-me up and a token of gratitude. But dammit, it had to be Marconi. I warned them up front not to buy Chinese food.

I had a guy on my team who lived near Marconi Pizza, and since it was too far to deliver, he started picking it up and bringing it to the office. Everything was good and I had my Marconi pizza. And then, one Friday, I walked in to find that my co-worker had brought Revolution Pizza.

"What is this?" I asked.

"We're sick of Marconi," my co-worker said. "We like the pizza lunches, but it can't always be Marconi. We wanted to switch it up." But Marconi is my *favorite*. I could probably eat it every day and never get sick of it. I begrudgingly put my own interests aside, and eventually the team settled on Maker Pizza, which I admit is really good, but it costs twice as much as Marconi—nearly a $180 for four pizzas.

Here we go again.

Can't Really Motivate 'em, and the Problems with CRMs

Customer Relationship Management (CRM) systems are both a blessing and a curse.

Since their inception, they've allowed for easy communication with customers, giving salespeople the chance to code customer interests and target their sales activities around those specific interests. Rather than just being a tool, CRM is a mindset and a way of doing business aimed at enhancing customer relationships and communications with your customers.

Why, then, have virtually all of the organizations I've worked for struggled so hard with adoption and utilization of CRM tools?

I readily admit I'm not a subject matter expert for all the popular CRMs out there, and many will boast about amazing results. I'm also not here to debate the benefits of a million-dollar integration of a high-end CRM into your company's back end. I approach this topic as an entrepreneur who's worked in 50 to 100-person companies, and these are the issues I've encountered. Hopefully my experiences will save you from pulling out your hair as some of these situations crop up.

Orders/Accounting System is Separate From the CRM

The number one problem, by far, that I've uncovered with CRM systems is a distinct break in the chain between the order/accounting system and the CRM sales management system.

Accounting systems that manage inventory and orders are typically not geared around the sales function, and vice versa. If you're starting from scratch, you should ensure that there's a tight integration between these systems.

The sales order and accounting team are concerned with what's written on customer purchase orders. Often, these never mention any of the people that may have spent months spec'ing out a system and driving a sale to completion. The order entry team is worried about getting the buyer's information correct for things like bill to address, ship to address, buyer's name and email, and tax IDs. They need to check and verify credit terms, shipping terms, items, configurations, prices, and discounts. This is typically completely isolated from all the fanfare around selling. Salespeople don't care about any of this and the systems where these orders are entered, and the accounting systems that bill and invoice are often distinctly separate from the CRM.

As recently as 2019, I was involved with deploying a new Enterprise Resource Planning (ERP) system in my latest business and was bound and determined to break the cycle and ensure the ERP system we chose had an embedded CRM. It did. We spent $250,000 deploying this software and were excited to finally have all our systems integrated. Prior to that we had four separate systems. One was for accounting, one for CRM, one for quoting, and another for inventory/order management. They all shared data in one way or the other, but it had become a pain point as our company grew.

It was not until we'd fully rolled out the software and started to use it that we uncovered what slipped past us during the demos. The CRM was integrated into the main program having its own tab, but was essentially a "bolt-on" that was only cosmetically attached. The CRM required dedicated input from the sales team to maintain, but the order team that dealt with buyers and logistics personnel were not in a position to maintain the CRM. As a result, only the order management and accounting data was rigorously entered and maintained. Different software, same problem, all over again.

Salespeople often forgot to add the most important people to the CRM. Therefore, much of the important pieces of key customer information were missing. Key new staff are often never added, email addresses and phone numbers are typically incomplete or missing. Our business is one of face-to-face to selling, and often the key activities are done on the phone, in person, or over email. The CRM would require redundant data entry to save facts twice.

Imagine a salesperson speaking to a key customer about some important technical specs on the phone. He promises to research and respond with the answers post haste. He follows up the call with numerous emails to vendors, staff engineers, and other experts. Once he has finally determined the solution required, he pens a brief summary email to the customer and attaches a technical note. Is the salesman now supposed to restate all of this for the CRM so some manager can review everything they were already cc'd on via email?

Opportunity Manager

The key for us in CRM is the opportunity manager, someone who tracks deals and their stage in the funnel. We reduced stages to the least number of choices possible and paid for a key feature I find indispensable. When our salespeople create a quote for a customer, it automatically adds an opportunity to the CRM and sets the probability at 10%. Their CRM dashboard shows 10% deals, which flags them that they have new opportunities needing further qualification. We assume any deal at 10% hasn't been touched by the rep. Their job is to ensure they open each 10% deal in the OM and set correct sales stage (for instance, 25% for qualification, 40% for negotiation, etc.) and the close date.

We started out with good intentions, asking reps to code all sales calls and phone calls, but ultimately we came to a few stark realizations:

1. No one really checked and reviewed these calls and phone call records.

2. Entry of this data was typically redundant to the activity.

For instance, imagine this scenario playing out. I'm on a call with one of my sales reps and I say, "Hey Bob, did you call Rick at AcmeTech Solutions about the new production tester?" He quickly offers, "I sure did, Glenn."

I pepper him with questions. "Excellent, how did it go? What did he have to say? Do you think he is going to recommend our unit?"

Bob says, "Further to your demands, I've entered all the notes from each call into the CRM and added all my thoughts and comments. Are you suggesting you didn't bother reading any of this before calling me?" And then he says for added benefit, "I also cc'd you on the summary email to Rick and his boss at AcmeTech, outlining our proposal and such. Didn't you get the email?"

Gulp. "Well, I see that email now. I hadn't read it yet. Sorry. And no, I didn't have a chance to read your CRM notes before calling you."

"If you aren't going to read the notes in the CRM, then why are we entering them?" Bob asks. "I could have made several more phone calls in the time it took to enter the notes nobody is reading."

In order for me to reinforce my directive that all meetings and calls were documented, I was thereby signing myself up for the task of being obligated to read everything prior to calling my reps. This just wasn't possible.

The Most Important Thing

In the end, I relented and decided what was most important was not how calls and meetings were documented, but rather that they happened. Every rep records notes and to-dos differently, depending on what works for them. What I do enforce is opportunity management. I need to see what deals are entering the funnel. This is a key measurable and is important that we track each new deal and also monitor closely what deals are at 65% or above closing in the near term. We use this data for advanced inventory purchasing and to plan our 30-, 60-, and 90-day outlook for bookings.

Again, I want to stress this section is not meant to be anti-CRMs. What's important is before you adopt any kind of CRM, you really need to map out the workflow for your business. We realized that our business is not well suited to one driven by CRMs and click funnels. Our business is done face to face in the trenches, and causing our salespeople to sit in the office doing data entry rather than be visiting customers diminishes their sales value.

Craig Walker's 'Cockpit'

This story wouldn't be complete without telling the story about Craig Walker and his "cockpit."

Craig was an outlier in CRM. He was hired in the 1990s as a regional sales manager supervising about six of our salespeople. Over the years, I've deduced through completely un-scientific, non-traceable methods that only one or two in every 10 people adopt an all-in attitude toward the CRM. They make everything fit the CRM, and CRM drives everything they do.

About two to three in 10 half-ass adopt CRM utilization, while the other five, even under threat of firing, never really get the thing working for them. Although we strictly enforce updating the funnel, the same specs of one to two, two to three, and five of 10 people apply in terms of the quality of the input. They may update things, but we often find reps making blanket changes to close dates to feign moving things along. In reality they're just preventing them showing up in the past.

Craig utilized a multi-monitor setup at his desk, which is quite common today, but back then when we worked together we literally thought this was a cockpit. It was enough screens worthy of flying a plane, and that's what we called it. He loved that cockpit so much he would never leave it.

Here is a very close example of what his work setup looked like. Remember, this was the late 1990s, so imagine the power consumption with all those monitors!

Photo Credit windowscentral.com

Craig did everything from the cockpit and was he on top of his CRM. At the time, he came on board we were using Act!, and he ended up switching over to our system from a competitive CRM called Goldmine.

He was convinced he'd created a new selling model, which could be guided from his multi-monitor cockpit with the latest CRM software and a phone so he could leave messages. He was so lazy, in fact, he couldn't type full words, and that's why he developed all these initialisms and acronyms to save time while typing.

Craig was the author of one of my favorite initialisms involving the status of a call: VMLMCB, or "voice mail left message to call me back." In plain English, it means "I called the customer and got their voicemail, so I left a message for them to call me back." Other call reports he did contained the derivation VMLM (voice mail left message) for calls that did not have a call to action for the recipient to call us back. He also loved to use the acronym ACSE, which stood for "avoiding calls, sent email." He was lazy and far too comfortable in his cockpit.

Ultimately we let him go because he just wasn't making it happen. He taught us all the important lessons that CRMs are great and all, but for companies like ours, getting out in front of customers is paramount. His legacy is we get to use his initialisms to save us time as we race from call-to-call booking orders!

Same Difference Factor—Chabuduo

The literal translation of the Chinese phrase *chabuduo* is "difference not much," but what it means in real life usage is "close enough."[21] I also loosely translate it to a saying I heard growing up in Ontario, "same difference" (which never made sense to me) that's used to express your belief that two or more things are essentially the same, in spite of apparent differences.

On a personal level, when someone says chabuduo it's usually positive, and it's a way of saying, "this is ok and practical." However, in a business environment it usually translates to a negative in terms of the results or impact of the decision to apply chabuduo to that situation.

Uses and Misuses

In day-to-day life, the concept of chabuduo can be quite helpful in diffusing a situation. Perhaps you're buying coffee and it comes $2.03 and you have two U.S. singles or a Canadian toonie and no other change. You dig through your pockets looking for a few pennies. "Not a problem," the server says. "It's no big deal," or chabuduo.

This can also be used for misuse of language. When someone says, "same difference" for "no difference," instead of correcting the person, it's chabuduo. However, if someone messes it up completely while trying to pull a "same difference," you should correct the situation. That's not close enough. That's not chabuduo.

Calling Out Substandard Quality

When it comes to professional applications of chabuduo, it implies something with a more negative connotation and is something to be watched for and avoided because it basically implies cutting corners to get

---

21   Erik Nilsson, "Trying to translate terms like *chabudo*, more or less," China Daily, updated November 20, 2020, http://www.chinadaily.com.cn/a/202011/20/WS5fb70377a31024ad0ba954ab.html.

something done faster or cheaper. The temptations to greatly reduce production costs are always on your mind, and if you're importing goods from China, it's important to ensure rigid production and quality standards, as it is possible for chabuduo to be applied.

For example, let's say you're printing red shirts by the thousands. The first batches come through looking great, but then a batch shows up and the color is slightly off. It's not the exact same shade of red. The prevailing attitude could be that the exact dye was not available, so they used something as close as possible. *Chabuduo*. This is one of the reasons why in some cases China quality standards differ from Western countries.

When you're sourcing goods from the Far East with an eye to seemingly save money and jack your profits you can't skip first principles. You need to visit the factory and monitor closely for the following issues to crop up:

- Insufficient quality control
- Overlooking mistakes
- Schedule changes without notice
- Making changes without approval
- Extending production times
- Delays in servicing products

If you have strict production requirements, make sure you state them clearly in writing, and upon visiting ensure they are understood before you pull the trigger and go into any deal. This includes key factors like colors, sizes, lead times, product schedules, and shipping methods. If you skip this step, you're liable to end up hearing "chabuduo" at the worst possible time. I also suggest for high-value shipments that a pre-shipment inspection is performed in order to avoid any problems. With all of the sourcing we do in China, there are times with certain items and issues we accept a chabuduo response, such as those times when we can be flexible on packaging methods.

If you ever want to compare this attitude in North America, the best one I've found is the saying, *close only counts in horseshoes and hand grenades.* Up-and-coming companies should keep these ideas in mind. You can't really understand the concept of chabuduo until you experience it. But being forewarned means being forearmed.

CHAPTER 17

HIGH NEED TO ADD VALUE

I see many young, insecure salespeople falling into a trap of *needing to be needed*. This individual sense of significance is rooted in group participating or some cause beyond themselves. Needing to be needed is one of our fundamental desires, as everyone wants to feel significant.

When we're in meetings, we can exhibit tendencies to show we play an important role. But at times these behaviors achieve the opposite and come across as annoying and misplaced. Oftentimes a more subdued approach is appropriate, and you should remain silent or ask questions to let the customer speak. When you're feeling the need to seem knowledgeable and jump in on every topic with your comments while talking over others or out of turn, it's an extremely frustrating trait. I call this HINAV (high need to add value) and should be replaced with better strategies like these:

1. **Appropriate attendance**: Only attend meetings where your presence is warranted. No unnecessary staff should be engaged in meetings.

2. **Good preparation**: Come prepared. Distribute or ask for agendas in advance. Prepare all your questions or points you will make.

3. **Identify all roles**: Be certain the roles of all your staff attending the meeting. Try to determine which customers will be present and why.

4. **Play to your strengths**: Stick to playing to your specific strengths when presenting. If you're the best presenter so be it, but when technical issues arise ask the technical prime to setup and respond. Listen carefully to others and assign responsibilities to the best person.

5. **Encourage others**: Share the stage and make sure you allow all relevant perspectives to come through. Encourage coworkers well suited to reply to speak up in case they're deferring to you. Ask others for their opinions.

6. **Positive body language**: Make sure you are dressed properly, well rested, and reflect a professional image with your body language. Sit up straight and act professional.

No Good Deed Goes Unpunished

The basic meaning behind the phrase "no good deed goes unpunished" is that your beneficial actions may often go unappreciated, and more importantly, are met with outright hostility. Further, if your good deeds are appreciated, they often lead to additional requests by the receiving person, so be careful what you give as much as you are careful what you wish for.

Many people will take advantage of your acts of kindness. They may believe they deserve something else (maybe they do, and maybe they don't). I've encountered many examples of no good deed going unpunished during my life. There was a time once when I agreed to take in someone's cat since they could no longer keep it. The cat belonged to the daughter of a guy I knew, Luke, and she was heading off to college. Despite loving this cat dearly, she had to give it up. They struggled to find a home for it, and one fateful day while I was speaking to Luke, he told me the cat was Himalayan. I already had two of them and they are my favorite breed, so I was open to taking in the cat.

I was surprised when I picked up the cat to find how big it was compared to my male and female cats, Coco and Chanel. This cat was *huge.*

But I said I would take the cat, and I packed him up and brought him home. The cat hid for the first day or so, which is normal, and slowly poked its head out on the second day and ate.

I closed off the basement to keep an eye on him, and on the third or fourth day the cat got out an open door and took off. It ran away and never came back.

Oh no, I thought.

I spent hours driving around searching for the cat, and it yielded nothing. I called the pound and searched endlessly, sick to death over it, but ultimately I never found a trace of it.

I felt horrible and wondered what I should do. I decided that since I rarely see Luke and didn't know his daughter, I was going to remain silent. But all the while, a horrible foreboding was welling up in me.

A few months later, I bumped into Luke and he cornered me. The first thing he asked was about the cat. *Well, umm.* I had to be honest at that point and told him what happened. The cat ran away and was never found. His reaction shocked me quite a bit and was not what I was expecting as he totally freaked out on me. He was super pissed off and made me feel like a righteous piece of shit for "killing his daughter's cat."

Over the years whenever I saw him, he would say, "Kill any cats lately?" To this day, I still bump into him every once in a while, and although he is no longer upset, he constantly refers to me as "Glenn, the guy who killed my cat," and I continue to have flashbacks of the stress I endured because I wanted to help.

Another example of this came in 1977, when I was 15 and my brother was 17—a licensed driver. We lived in Niagara Falls, Ontario, just across the U.S. and Canadian border, and our parents ran a motel on Lundy's Lane, a famous tourist strip.

That winter, we headed to Kissing Bridge ski resort in Glenwood, New York, near Buffalo, normally about an hour's drive south. This spot was popular with Canadians because of the longer runs and steeper slopes. We all loved skiing there.

The day we arrived happened to be day one of the infamous blizzard of '77. If you weren't there and didn't experience that storm, it's hard to explain how devastating that storm was for the Niagara region of southern Ontario and western New York, which included the city of Buffalo. The blizzard was so intense, people literally froze to death in their vehicles because they couldn't make it to safety.

Some of the snow drifts were nine meters deep. Snow piles reached the tops of telephone poles and buried cars, making transportation nearly impossible for days. It was called by many the blizzard of the century.

As we left Kissing Bridge, the snow started and was coming down heavy. As the cars started getting stuck in the snow, my brother and his friend Dave got out of the car to help. I still call them heroes to this day, as I remember watching them push cars out of the snow and help people get on their way.

By the time they returned to the car, the roads were impassable. We were told we needed to head to the fire station in town. We were stranded for days, but on the bright side, we met a kind woman named Mrs. Parker, or Jenny as she asked us to call her, who fed us and introduced us to the sounds of Stevie Wonder and his iconic album *Songs in the Key of Life,* which had been released months earlier on Tamla Records. To this day, songs like "Sir Duke" and "Isn't She Lovely" bring back memories of how bad snow can be and how no good deed goes unpunished.

And this factor wouldn't be complete without a sales-related example. You don't need to go far in sales to find examples of these, and they all boil down to learning to take a breath before you jump into saying yes. In my opinion, there need to be bona fide benefits to you as well over and above being a nice guy or helping people out. I recall many times throwing in free options to sweeten a deal, only to then have customers suggest they should get free accessories to support the options as well.

For instance, you agree to offer the turbo model and the customer then suggests we should be obliged to provide better tires to support the increased horsepower and torque. Always carefully consider how these favors will be received and how the customer will perceive you. For instance, one time I sold a customer two different instruments. We offered the three-year warrantee for free to sweeten the deal as it was competitive. The third time rolled around and they literally said to us, "So, we assume the three-year warrantee will be thrown in free?" You get the idea.

It's Easier to Drown in the Deep End of the Pool

This trap is easy to set for yourself, and it's a reminder to be mindful of your communication approach so you don't wind up *un-selling your product.* In many ways, this lesson correlates with the need to avoid talking for more than a minute straight without directly asking or answering a question.

Imagine you're working with a customer and have a chance to pitch your wares, but in the simplest of terms, your product is not one the customer clearly has a need for at the outset. You're convinced your product or service can help them, but for the last 10 years, these guys have done the heavy lifting themselves or essentially lived without such tools. They're blind to the productivity enhancements or leverage your tools provide. Let's use the example of a CRM solution tied into your website that tracks pages users visit, time spent on the site, and sends reminders when shopping carts are abandoned before a purchase is made.

You get the audience and begin asking questions. This can often happen when you get a referral and the potential client is clueless as to why they would want to work with you. Or perhaps, you met them at a trade show and were able to book a brief meeting with the client. They may have a sense something isn't working in the area your company focuses on, but frankly, they need you more than they realize. To set the stage for real engagement, you ask, "Hey Bob, do you guys ever find customers filling up their shopping cart and then abandoning the cart midway and never checking out?" Bob lights right up and says, "You have no idea. If I had a dollar for every cart that was left open, I'd be a millionaire."

You latch on to this and say, "Well that's great, Bob. I think you'll be excited. If we can show you how our tool is helping companies like yours to flip 20% to 30% of abandoned carts into sales, would you be interested in a trial?"

"Damn straight I would."

"That's excellent. You're going to be blown away!"

This is where you should end the preliminary meeting and move to lock them in for a trial, but you don't. Rather you press on, and at this point you do the unthinkable and start discussing too many problems and features at once. "In addition to resolving the cart issue, we also provide integrated Linux server back-end integration to the cloud, with gigabyte connectivity to your web services. This provides nano adjusted service sliced offset program support. I'm sure you've struggled from time to time with lag and offset coding errors? Our solution uses the latest Spike Flash code. Let me show you a few slides on that."

At this point, the death knell rings. "Oh wow, Jack! I had no idea about the complexity of these plug-ins," Bob says. "I was sold at shopping carts but honestly, this is way above me and I'm going to have to point you to our director of IT and software solutions. He's traveling for a month doing systems reviews at a bunch of sister offices, but I'm sure he'll be interested in hearing all about this when he's back. I'll introduce you. Thanks for coming by. I need to get back to the lobby. There's a guy there waiting for me who keeps selling me stuff."

In essence, you dragged this guy into the deep end of your technical pool and literally drowned them. This is a classic sales mistake. Salespeople are obsessed with going deep into product explanations. You need to discover their specific identified need, ask a couple probing questions for other challenges, and then focus. Don't overdo it. Remember, there's no perfect formula, but you should do your best to use common sense. The ideal number of questions should lead to discussing two to three customer problems during one sales call. Stick to the rule of three and it's tough to go wrong.

Stolen Dreams: Multi-Port Disaster

I pride myself on finding creative solutions for customer problems and leveraging customers and partners to help create something where the whole is greater than the sum of its parts. My first example of a solution sell was back in the mid 1990s. This will seem rudimentary in terms of connectivity today, but at the time it was groundbreaking, and I can claim full credit for the concept.

We had a customer, a small regional CLEC (Competitive Local Exchange Carrier) that offered services at various points in Canada and specialized in T1- and T3-type data connections. These were expensive dedicated pipes between offices that companies relied upon for connecting IT systems. This CLEC was responsible for monitoring and ensuring up time for these connections, and some of them were provisioned using wireless microwave links in difficult to reach places, and were subject to some downtime. They bought instruments from us that monitored the T1 or T3 traffic and recorded any outages. They also had to dispatch technicians to these sites and tear off a paper tape from the unit, bring it back to HQ, and decide what credits were due for outages. In some cases, they used helicopters to reach these locations. The entire affair was an ordeal and very expensive.

I approached a local software shop in Toronto and proposed an idea. Could we create a system using two PCs and a modem that allowed the remote PC to connect to the recorder output and record the results and compile into a table? The local PC at headquarters would dial up daily and download the reports. They would no longer need to read the paper tape or go there at all to change the paper. The software worked flawlessly and the Remote ME3401A Digital Transmission Analyzer (see below) was created. We sold numerous systems and CLEC never had to fly in and change the paper tape again.

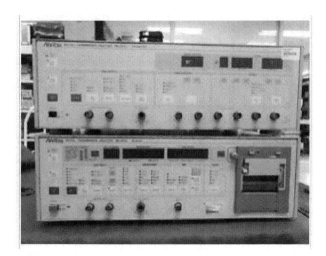

The more significant impact of this was how it affected the overall company. Based on my much-touted success with creating a third-party system by adding instruments and third-party custom-written software, the company went all in on a systems division. The original software person I contracted was hired on a much larger scale basis and the entire North American sales team was now pushing custom systems.

My next invention was something I was super proud of and became what was called a *multi-port test system*. It essentially used a high-speed electronic switch with multiple inputs and outputs connected to a single tester. This allowed the users to scan and test four, eight, and 16 channels at the same time. We worked with an important customer of mine and as the system began to take shape, a large military contractor in Boston took notice and began to buy them before I could even get my first order. I believe they ended up with probably 20 of these MPTS units valued at over $100,000 each. This was nice business, and due to custom nature of the unit, it was hard for a competitor to displace us.

However, the real problem occurred with my customer, and this became a painful lesson. We flew the client to Boston, rented a car, and took them to our other customer to see the system in action. We entertained them and fed them and made sure they were 1000% happy with the way our system worked before we headed back to Ontario, Canada with the hopes of some great business.

The customer ultimately decided they were going to buy three or four systems. We prepared our quote and presented it with much fanfare while we waited for our half-million-dollar order to roll in. At some point, the senior manager of the test group called me in for a meeting. I raced down there to see what was up and bring back my order. Upon arriving, I could tell immediately something was gravely wrong. He had a senior procurement person sitting in the meeting too who I had never met, and they dropped the bomb on me shortly afterwards.

"As you know, Glenn, we have a deal with another supplier of test equipment, and it's our obligation to give them the right of last refusal on all test equipment purchases," they said.

"Well, this is a custom test solution, not a standalone item, and they have nothing that compares at all," I said.

"You're right, Glenn," they responded. "You see, there was fanfare around your unit and they got wind of it. In the end, they pressured us and we capitulated. They're willing to also write a custom software solution and combine all their instruments in the same way to do the same multi-port tests."

I was shocked.

"So, you're allowing them to copy our solution we designed for you? We spent countless hours figuring out all these subtleties, only for you to pass all that inside knowledge of how we did it to them?"

"Umm, well, yes. We know it sucks, but our hands are tied."

This amounted to the worst possible loss of my sales career. Many will argue some of the finer points and even my justification for being upset. The real issue for me was the fact that this kind of test was unknown. I came up with the idea, had programmers pull everything together to make it work, and the customer allowed a competitor access.

We went on to sell many systems in the United States and elsewhere, but the sting I felt from this betrayal is still fresh today. Protect your IP and ideas however you can.

Always Ask for the Order

I feel almost like I'm plagiarizing a million other books when I suggest asking for the order, but seriously, how can any book be written without addressing this most basic and important tenet of selling? Always Be Closing (ABC) is something every salesman should follow religiously. In this regard, *Glengarry Glen Ross* got quite a few things right, including letting everyone know that coffee is for closers.

If you're not closing, you're not selling.

Everything in the world of selling is all about getting the customer to continue along a series of continuous and escalating steps that lead them to say yes. No is your enemy.

Beyond ABC, Alec Baldwin's character Blake in *Glengarry Glen Ross* also highlighted another acronym to the salesmen: A.I.D.A., or attention, interest, decision, and action.

Do you have the customer's *attention*? Sending form emails and leaving lazy voicemail messages are not generating attention. These are the modes of communication that cause someone to push that delete button. It's a lot easier to get their attention, and keep it, when you get in front of them.

Once you have their attention, you can move to the next step, which is *interest*. Again, interest is not something you pray for—it's something you earn and maintain. You need to show your product and service in the best possible light. Apply your GBL before you visit customers for presentations and use it to focus your attention on what will get their interest. Don't memorize useless facts that can easily be referenced in the manual, data sheet, or FAQ. Focus on the killer app feature your product's designer built into it. Show those features that competitors will have trouble showing a match for in a whiz bang presentation.

Once you have their attention and interest, you need to move them along the spectrum toward making a *decision*. If you have shown them everything they need to see and it meets their needs, you need to close. This is the time when you get them to make a decision and take *action*.

I've watched the key scenes from *Glengarry Glen Ross* a bunch of times, and admittedly, aspects of the movie today are borderline politically incorrect. The Alec Baldwin speech is harsh and insensitive. "Close, it's yours. If not, you're going to be shining my shoes." But let me ask you this. If you were a doctor wanting to be a surgeon, would you expect to be handled with kid gloves, knowing one slip of the knife and your patient dies? No, this is a tough game, and only closers win. Everyone else gets left behind.

CHAPTER 18

CALL AT LEAST SEVEN TIMES

The marketing rule of seven states that a prospect needs to hear your message at least seven times before they'll take action. You also need to remember these rules when calling customers:

1. Over 90% of all customer interactions happen over the phone.

2. It takes an average of seven cold call attempts to reach a prospect.

3. In a typical company with 100 to 500 employees, an average of seven people are involved in most buying decisions.

4. Create other ways of contacting customers to accelerate the rule of seven, such as social media sites like LinkedIn.

5. You're not being a nag if you're communicating effectively. You're being effective.

6. After you call, leave a voicemail and send an email.

7. Use social media to enhance your image.

8. Use email systems to send automated messages and newsletters.

Albert Martin Demo

The Albert Martin is burned into my brain as one of the most shocking and surprising sales calls I've ever been on.

At my first job in technical sales, we all practiced the fine art of greed-based learning (GBL). We sold upwards of 50 manufacturers' products and they were all very technical instruments with complicated functions and features. It was virtually impossible to know them all well, and although we could spout off key parameters for a customer, we would typically bring in factory reps to do serious demos that were beyond our level of knowledge.

Albert Martin was the expert on logic analyzers, emulators, and all the microprocessor test type products. I was responsible for a handful of vendors as well including digital storage oscilloscopes (DSOs), power supplies, electronic loads, and also this very cool line of EPROM (Erasable Programmable Read Only Memory) programmers. EPROM chips retain their data even when the chip's power supply is switched off.

We could never learn how to demo all of these items ourselves, so we would share the load and help each other out on calls. Albert would come on calls with me when the vendors were not able to accompany us, and I would do the same for Albert. There were five of us in the Greater Toronto Area (GTA), and we used this approach between us to balance our workload and quota and still support each other.

One fine day, I was traveling to the outer reaches of Scarberia, which is what we call Scarborough, a suburb of Toronto that's akin to Siberia because the traffic and routes to get there from the west end of the city were always a headache. We arrived at the customer with the programmer in hand and were escorted to the second floor. As we ferried through the building, I was sure we had the factors *never forgetting a face* and *something in our hand and something in our mind* covered—namely a nice demo and a killer proposal for when it came time to close. But even so, something seemed amiss.

Albert made small talk with the client while I set up the demo. For some reason, the customer seemed off. We were unwelcome and he was reluctant. As I started to get into my whiz-bang presentation, the client started in with all of this talk about a competitive brand, Data I/O, a leading global provider of advanced data and security programming solutions. I knew right away we were clearly in the number two position, and number one was an 800-pound gorilla and faraway the market leader. However, we had an advantage they couldn't compete against. For standard market chips that anyone could program and where there was a need to do them in bulk, we had a clear price advantage. Our product was half the price and had a speed and number of simultaneous chips capacity. However, the difference was like Cadillac was to Pontiac. If you could afford a Cadillac, why wouldn't you buy one?

As we rolled along and I was showing all of the EPROM features, the client wouldn't let up. *Data I/O does this, and Data I/O does that, and Data I/O is bigger than you, and Data I/O is better than you.* It was super annoying to listen to. As the client blathered on, Albert grabbed the power cord while standing about five feet away from the wall socket, and literally tears the cord out of the wall and it whiplashes past my head. Then he addressed the client.

"I've decided a couple things," Albert told him. "One, we're not demoing this product to you, and two, you can't buy it from us. Glenn, pack up the demo. We're leaving."

The client began fumbling and mumbling his words. "What's wrong? What did I say?" he asked.

"You have no intention of buying our unit," Albert said. He glanced at me and nodded, repeating his earlier directive for the benefit of the customer. "Pack up. We're not doing the demo and we're definitely *not* selling a unit to this customer. I refuse to sell it to him." The client continued muttering, trying to fix things. This was clearly a first for him. God knows it was a first for me! I sheepishly wrapped the cord as I wondered what was going to happen next.

As the client continued asking for clarity, Albert told him, "Look, we're not some door-to-door salesmen that came here to waste time and try to sell you something you don't need. You invited us here, probably because your boss asked you to do your due diligence and look at more than one brand, and not just buy the most expensive Cadillac unit. However, you clearly are biased and have no intention of giving anyone else a shot at this business. What you don't realize is this is one of those times that despite wanting the fancy brand name, we all know there are clear-cut reasons to buy our unit, especially since you're doing standard chips in bulk.

"I understand for your development unit you probably need the competition, but why would you spend four times as much for a slower unit in production? Regardless, it doesn't matter. You have disrespected me and my colleague, and I have decided we are *not* selling you a unit."

With that, the tide started to shift, and the client started acting reticent about his hostile behavior. The unit we were (not) offering quickly became the forbidden fruit. His cocky, arrogant tone faded away and FOMO (fear of missing out) kicked in. Like Dr. Robert Cialdini's famous scarcity principle, our product now had more value to the client because it was unavailable to him.

Now that the client realized he had offended us, disrespected us, and been removed as a possible candidate, his attitude changed. "I'm sorry about my behavior," he said. "I didn't mean to seem hostile or unwelcoming, and I do value you spending the time coming over here to do the demo. Can we start over and do this again?" Albert looked at me as if he was weighing the odds and non-verbally checking if I was ok.

"Ok, fine. Let's start again," Albert said. So I returned to showing the unit, zeroing in on the key parameters that worked in our favor—namely the larger capacity, faster speed, and lower price. We were given a chance to reiterate that for bulk production, and we actually had an advantage despite not being the shiniest brand on the street.

In the end, the customer agreed. They ultimately designed our unit into their production process and bought eight units from us, which at the time was an amazing sale.

Bobby Watson Discount Strategy

I constantly struggle with this factor and often wonder if I should apply it, and if so, how. I also gauge when it may be applied to me. Using the factor feels, admittedly, a little misleading. But, at the same time, it can mean the difference between nominal gross margin sales and a more profitable one. It gets used by customers all the time, and often we're required to deploy it because the customer has deployed the same tactic on us and we need to salvage the margin.

The Bobby Watson—named after my first sales manager —is deployed at the end of a sales cycle and only once the sale for your firm is won and the customer purchase order is in hand. This means you clearly and without a doubt have a firm PO from your customer. There's nothing in your way of completing the sale, but due to various maneuverings of the sales process, you will often find yourself and your margins beat to a pulp.

Before we proceed, it's important to explain gross margin, and the difference between markup and margin.

Markup (Price Spread)

Markup is the difference between the selling price of a good or service and cost. It's often expressed as a percentage over the cost. A markup is added into the total cost incurred by the producer of a good or service in order to cover the costs of doing business and create a profit. Thus, the difference between the cost of a product or service and its sale price is called the markup. It's often cause for much confusion as it relates to the key business metric of gross margin. In mathematical terms, the formula looks something like this: Markup = Sale Price – Cost.

Gross Margin

Gross margin is the difference between revenue and cost of goods sold (COGS), divided by revenue. Gross margin is expressed as a percentage. Generally, it's calculated as the selling price of an item, less the cost of goods sold (e. g. production or acquisition costs, not including indirect fixed costs like office expenses, rent, or administrative costs), then divided by the same selling price. Gross margin is often used interchangeably with gross profit, however the terms are different. Gross profit is a monetary amount and gross margin is a percentage or ratio.

If you're running a sales company with an average margin of 20% and you have customers pulling a Bobby Watson on you to the tune of two to three percent on every order, your operating margin will drop to 17%. Margin is what you use to pay salaries, expenses, and other costs, and the rest becomes earnings (i.e. EBITDA), and ultimately net profit. In this example, the operating margin is reduced by 3%/20% = 15% reduction. Uneducated salespeople might think, "What's the big deal? It's only two or three percent, and it will get me the deal!"

But depending on your expense levels, this reduction could quickly drive your net profits to zero.

A Bobby Watson works like this. Once the order is in hand, you call the supplier and tell them you're down to the wire and confident you can deliver them an order without delay. But in addition to the last-minute discounts you've given, you also need the supplier to kick in two to five percent to bring this deal home. The key is to present this as a shared pain strategy, and in many cases it is, you may have discounted at the last minute to secure the PO you have in hand.

You let the supplier know these discounts are shared and are also absorbing a large dent in your margin. Confident the sale is minutes away if you can get this extra little kicker, the conversation might typically go something like this: "Hey Bob, it's Glenn from Acme Marketing. As you know, our sales guy Sam has been working for weeks to close the deal with MajorCo and we're at the final round on this one and they're hammering us hard. They're threatening to send us a PO today and claim we are the preferred choice, but they just can't justify the price in comparison to the B brand. If you want the deal, you need to drop five percent and offer free shipping to our location out west. We're willing to absorb two percent of this and we need to ask if you can throw in three percent and drop ship for us to their location instead of shipping to us first." If the supplier goes for this strategy (and they often will), you'll have increased your profit margin significantly. See the example below:

Bobby Watson Gross Margin Increase

	Normal Deal	Bobby Watson
Sell Price:	$20,000	$20,000
Freight:	$400	$0 (free)
Cost:	$15,000	$14,400 (three percent extra discount)
Total COGS:	$15,400	$14,400
Margin	$4,600 (23%)	$5,600 (28%)

In the example above, the extra three-percent discount and free freight your company will enjoy (28-23)/23 = 22% more margin!

The technique can be further enhanced if deployed at the 11th hour of the suppliers' month, quarter, or year end. Often they're trying to hit a number and this can be just the motivation required to squeeze this last five percent or more out of your supplier. I call this delaying of the maneuver until the last possible moment as *slow Bobby Watson*. More often than not, the supplier will capitulate and offer the discount or some portion thereof. This extra discount can be considered pure profit.

If the supplier offers the discount, wait 15 to 30 minutes and then send in the PO with the newly agreed-upon lower price and reap the enhanced profit margin. Naturally, you can't pull this off on every deal. Therefore, you always save this for deals that have been costly for you or where the supplier wouldn't share in the competitive deal and they're content to let you shoulder the discounting to secure a deal yourself. I call this tactic on their part pulling the famous *deep pockets with short arms* routine, as the manufacturers who we deal with are always dealing with healthier margins than we ever get.

If they pull the *deep pockets with short arms* routine on you, then barring any need for rush delivery, you can delay placing your order with the supplier and let the minutes of the month or quarter tick closer and closer to the end and do a full-scale slow Bobby Watson until their anxiety builds and builds until they ultimately relent. If not, it's time to use *the Carolina*, which is an offshoot of the Bobby Watson.

The Carolina

This strategy is regularly applied by procurement staffs that have orders on their desk that need to be placed with a specific supplier. There's no question where the PO is being sent. You need to buy from a specific supplier and the draft POs are prepared.

Where the Bobby Watson is deployed by salespeople, the buyers demanding the last five percent from you is using *the Carolina*. This is a very soft approach, and I recommend deploying it whenever possible. The technique involves the buyer contacting the order entry people who normally accept the POs with a request.

"I have a few orders to send your way and it totals over $20,000," the buyer says. "Look, for this magnitude of orders, I need you to do something extra for me. The transportation costs are killing me, and the customers have beaten us up on the deals."

Essentially, you need to offer any plausible reason you having been "beat up" and show you need help. Given we're in Canada, one possible scapegoat is the exchange rates from USD to CAD.

"Can you find an extra two to three percent on this package deal for us?" the buyer asks. It's also worth asking if they can do free freight as well, since freight could cost one and a half to three percent of the purchase amount. The supplier can't really argue with your reasons, even if they disagree. They can refuse your requests but they can only listen to you at this point. As with many things in life, you won't know unless you ask. When the salespeople fail pulling off a Bobby Watson on their sales contracts, your buyers are going to deploy the Carolina. Because in the end, even one percent more on a 20% deal is actually raising your margins by five percent!

CHAPTER 19

DOFASCO FACTOR

This is one of the best lessons I ever learned, and my first boss in sales taught it to me. We were trying to sell products to a steel plant in Hamilton, Ontario. So many steel towns across Canada and the United States have gray skies and smoke stacks. Everyone works in the mills, and entire towns are centered around them.

Back in the day when you visited one of these steel plants, you didn't even have to check into security. If you knew your way around the plant (maybe you took a mini-tour the last time you visited) you could drive around, park outside the mill, walk across gangways, go through doorways, and up stairwells to find the engineer who managed all that equipment that was keeping the mill running properly. Looking back today, how would you even get on the property? Eventually security cracked down, and you'd have to check in first before stopping by. But in those earlier days, when there was a lot of freedom of movement in plants, I learned so many lessons.

One of these lessons occurred when I was the sales lead on a digital oscilloscope product—it's an instrument we sold that displays signal voltages. I went in and I talked to the engineer and tried to drum up the business for this product but was told they were actually deploying this cold rolling technology, a different way for Dofasco to produce steel instead of a hot-rolling process.

The state-of-the-art process was being installed by Toshiba, as it was a Toshiba steel mill.

I realized that the engineer I was meeting not only wanted to buy one of these oscilloscopes, but he also wanted to buy electronic measuring recorders and other devices. They needed so many instruments, and even some that we didn't sell.

That's when the lightbulb turned on.

I went back to Bobby Watson, the company owner and a consummate salesman, and explained the situation. "Not only do they want to buy a scope (which was a $4,000 instrument), but they're also buying dozens and dozens of instruments to measure signals throughout this new steel mill," I told him. "They're looking at buying old style strip chart recorders and want to install them to monitor the most advanced steel mill in the world."

"Well, we have to go back there, right?" he said.

Bobby possessed GBL combined with an incredible selling capability. And I wanted to learn. Our new instrument could measure and store and display signals digitally, which was a big upgrade from the old strip chart recorder that involved a pen and a piece of paper. *So,* I thought, *Why don't we show them all the new items, the latest stuff?* We started kicking down the doors to show them what we had to offer. Every time we would meet someone, they would say, "Yeah, this is very cool." But they'd also say, "It's not really my decision. You have to talk to the line manager."

This is normally where I would probably have gotten caught up asking for the line manager's contact information and following up with him over the phone. Bobby Watson wasn't having any of that.

"Ok, what's his name and number?" Bobby asked. The technician we were meeting with gave him the information.

Bobby followed up with another question. "Ok, is he here at work today? Is he here now?"

"Yes."

"Good. Take us to him right now. Hand-deliver us. Introduce us. Let's get this all in the open."

Bobby Watson got the technician to walk us through the plant to find this line manager. We sold the next guy, one of many people we ended up having to meet at Dofasco over the course of a day or two. Then we found out they couldn't install any of the instruments without Toshiba signing off.

"Ok, who's the exact person with Toshiba who will have to say yes to this?" Bobby Watson asked.

Toshiba is a global behemoth. Did we have to fly to Japan to sell some person? After a fair amount of back and forth, we ended up getting the name of the general manager of Toshiba's Toronto division and got the contact. We drove straight from Dofasco to meet the GM. There were no delays. We didn't stop for coffee, we didn't go to lunch. We got in the car and we drove, and all the while Bobby was coaching me up, explaining how we were going to get the GM to sign off on this, and then we were going to go back to Dofasco and get the order. Lo and behold, we went and talked to this GM, a ginormous man who towered over my five-six frame. This guy was six-five huge.

When you think of Toshiba sending someone to make sure they don't fuck up a steel mill, this was the guy you'd picture. I was 28 years old at the time, and even though I was intimidated, to my boss's and customer's amazement, I was able to GBL this completely different product into pole position against this recording technology that they've been using for years. It wasn't rocket science—I didn't cure cancer or anything, but it was a to-tally new way of using these kinds of scopes that the customer and my boss would have never considered. I convinced them to do away with paper tape and learn to access and store all these digital channels remotely.

My boss could have kicked me out of the way and taken the deal be-cause he knew how big it was, but he also needed me to deliver. He was also generous with his time and skills. We got the giant Toshiba GM to agree, then we planned to go back to Dofasco to get them to sign off.

"No, you can't do that," he said.

"Why not?"

"The entire deal's brokered through Guillevin International." They were the giant electric company that put in all the electrics and was responsible for all the instruments.

"Well, what do we have to do?" we asked.

"You have to go see the team at Guillevin, and get them to sign off on it and make the purchase. You can't get a PO from Dofasco directly on this one." It turned out they were in Mississauga, another city located about half an hour away by car.

I swear to God, we drove straight from Toshiba's office in Toronto to Guillevin's office in Mississauga. We cold-called and walked straight in the door, didn't make an appointment, and asked to speak to the person whose approval we needed.

Guillevin International was basically a giant version of us. They sold all kinds of electronic wires and controls and mechanisms, and they also sold to installations of $100 million steel plants. We went through all the technologies and kind of got the buy-off on it, but then there were all sorts of negotiations. But in the end, we got the guy we needed to agree to it as well.

In the course of 48 hours, we drove all across Southern Ontario getting all of these high-ranking people at different companies to sign off on the deal. This was 1991, and one purchase order was for $500,000 of instruments. My whole quota for the year was somewhere around $750,000 or $900,000, so this deal was damn near my whole quota.

We were able to change the customer's mind on the technology that he thought he needed. The part that was mind blowing to me, and that I still reflect on today, is that when someone tells you, "Oh, I like it, but you've gotta talk to the foreman," I don't go back to the office to figure out how I'm going to get to the foreman. I say, "Ok, great, introduce me now. Take me over there right now and introduce me." And if they don't have enough time, I'll come back. There's just no time like the present.

You Can't Teach an Old Dog How to do New Tricks
Correctly

Over the last 35 years of running sales companies, I've learned a few tricks. Some are straightforward, as the message behind *never fax the facts or ship the shit* is pretty obvious.

The issue here is more subtle. With each decade, technology advances at a breakneck pace. With each advance we adopt high-tech in a big way, and to put it mildly, we have a number of people who can't or won't keep up with the changes. It's not fair to say it's the older generation, because that's just not true. I'm one of the oldest in the company and I adopt new technology usually without issue. Regardless of age, many people struggle to adapt new technology *properly*. That is the crux of this issue.

Many of our staff loosely sign up for the new technology and learn the basics. But two levels of problems quickly emerge. First, they fail to keep up with the technology, struggle with the training, or they're fearful of the unknown—typically because they feel they're expected to jump into new technological territory without appropriate knowledge or support. Secondly, and more to the issue for me, is they don't adapt to the new technology.

For instance, imagine you're rolling out a formal LinkedIn sales strategy for prospecting new customers with your senior account managers. You pay for everyone to upgrade to the Navigator premium level and set them up with logins for the training. In short order you come to realize half the team didn't get the memo. They still haven't updated their profile to the current standards of what's expected. They're still using LinkedIn as a lookup tool for customer names to add to their contact list in Outlook or the CRM.

They haven't made the transition to a new mindset of social selling. They can't change gears when they realize it's not just about adding new contacts to your list. It's about making those interactions meaningful. It's about evolving your entire brand to build trust and loyalty using a new social selling method.

Instead of dialing for dollars, you need the reps to use social media to connect with prospects, develop a social connection with them, and build engagement. Modern relationship-building can replace outdated cold calling strategies. However, people are intransigent and don't even realize it. In their mind, they're thinking "WTF, boss! I'm using LinkedIn. How do you think I found Bob at TechNor Innovations?" Then there's grumbling and huffing and puffing, wondering what *your* issue is.

Here are some tips I've developed to not only train your old dogs, but to also have them make the true leap of faith to a new way doing things:

1. *Find a key executive to champion the new tools.* Whether it's the CEO, VP of sales, or a director, you need an executive who has influence to sponsor the program and provide a voice for the company during the rollout of new technology.

2. *Have the executive sponsor explain why you're adopting the new technology.* Have them show staff using real world examples and explain how the new platform will benefit the company and the sales reps. The sponsor may also need to get sideliners on board. For instance, they may say, "I don't use social media, period." Well, that's fine on your own time, but for the company profile, you need one. Consider it a business account and do what you want personally, but everyone needs a LinkedIn, Twitter, and Instagram account at a minimum.

3. *Training is often expensive but critical.* You need to adapt the training to all levels of staff. There will be myriad expertise levels to deal with and you need to address them all. Also, don't make the mistake of using only one method to train people. I don't believe in online-only training. Some may prefer online training sessions while others need face-to-face in-person training, or the support of a personal coach.

4. *Find a staff level champion.* Don't just pick the tech geek who was born getting all this stuff. You need to spread around the champion badges between technical experts, influencers, and other savvy team members. Having some staff spread the excitement is infinitely more powerful in driving adoption than a memo demanding it from the CEO.

5. *Roll out the program stages.* Don't go all in right away. As much as possible, break down the rollout, learn from mistakes and challenges, and then incorporate improvements into the project. As modules start to show some payoff bring on more advanced portions of the tool.

6. *Create a company community for sharing successes and tips.* There's no better tip for getting others to adopt something than to share success stories. This showcases the person and drives demand amongst others and demonstrates the value of the new technology.

7. *Use the technology in all areas of the business.* Don't just force this on the sales team while every other department continues to flounder with old methods.

There's no doubt technology and changes are here to stay, but so are people, and you need talented people to grow your business. You can't build a sales team for the 2020s and beyond without both. Make sure you develop the strategies to get the right technology in place, and then train and motivate them to use it right.

Discount to Increase Factor

Everyone loves a bargain. Just check out the insanity on Black Friday or Boxing Day, when people show up in the middle of the night for a spot at the front of the line so they can snag the best deal.

We all find ourselves going for all the discount incentives out there designed to drive up the RPE (revenue per engagement). Once the customer is buying, the key is to maximize the revenue in the transaction, as you can't predict when they'll be back again.

The best way to drive up RPE is promotional and discounted pricing. Discounts will bring in new customers who've never worked with you and encourage them to try out products. There are many ways to offer a discount and they all have strengths and weaknesses. The key is to find the best pricing model for your business so you can maximize growth. In keeping with setting prices (see the Wittson price factor example), there are myriad ways to offer discounts, some better than others. Here are some discount methods you can use to drive business:

New Customer Sign-up Discount

It goes without saying that acquiring customers is expensive and time consuming. One of the easiest ways to attract new customers is to offer a new customer discount or promotion. The way we do this is to offer a coupon for X% off certain brands on our webstore, or free shipping, etc. This gives customers a reason to switch from a brand they're already using.

No Risk Try and Buy

For my company, this strategy involves leaving a unit with a customer for 30 days in the field. There's no risk to the customer, but if after the 30 days the unit is performing as promised, the customer agrees to issue a PO for the full amount. It's important for the *try and buy* that a list of key objectives are set. If not, the try and buy can become a crutch for salespeople to use to get units in the door hoping the customer will find reasons to buy it. This is how we avoid money back guarantee clauses, as the types of products we sell are typically not sold in the manner of retail goods.

To further jack up the effectiveness, once the customer has committed to a purchase after the try and buy, we offer further options for them to consider, such as:

- Adding software and hardware options not in the base unit

- Extended warranties and service contracts with the manufacturer

- Flexible payment terms, such as lease to own

Limited-Time Promotions

This is a very popular method we use to encourage customers to pull the trigger, and often use it to push our supplier partners to participate as well. When using this strategy, we'll contact a top supplier and say, "Look, we know we're in your final quarter for the fiscal year. Let's do a 90-day promotion." This way, we'll both give up some discount and offer the customer a 20% discount time-limited to the end of June, for instance. This is how we create demand with the customer and a sense of urgency or a takeaway. Although we don't do a lot of subscriptions in our business, when we do have software or service items sold on subscription we position the discount to expire at the end of the month and state that it won't be repeated, which can clearly motivate customers to take action. In short, the idea is to invoke the scarcity fear that they could lose out and prompt them to take action.

Competitive Discounts

These can be vital when competing in the world with customers like David Gleason. You cannot ignore the fact of competition, especially when customers can Google and compare at the click of their mouse. It's vital you check your facts and research competitors' offerings so you know you're competitive. One thing we do is Google a broad range of part numbers and look at the prices that come up from competitors on a basic search. We use these prices to develop a concept called MAP, or minimum advertised price. Sometimes the MAP is set by the manufacturer, which makes it easy to determine how low you can go with online pricing. However, deploying the same strategy on prices that aren't controlled ensure that when people Google that part number, the price displayed online for us is equal to or lower than other competitors.

Overstocked Discount or Freebies

Given we're a distributor, our goal is to sell from stock. There are some manufacturer's items we sell that are nearly impossible to stock because of the purchase configurations. But our business strategy is to sell from stock wherever possible—meaning we're making sizable investments in the manufacturer's stock to ensure we have the popular items on the shelf and available for immediate shipment. Not everything sells, and only some items can be returned or stock rotated.

This causes the dreaded condition of overstock, which eats into a company's profits as the value of this inventory declines over time and ultimately must be written off. There are also tax implications in some places on the value of stock held at year end. To that end, getting rid of stale or slow-moving stock is of paramount concern. This is why it's important to develop strategies to include products that are about to expire or will be soon be discontinued. If someone is buying an instrument for testing, we'll often add in stock test cables to the quote. This is a *would you like fries with that* strategy, but we often discount these items when the real goal is to sell some slow-moving stock.

Event or Seasonal Discount

At my current firm, we've deployed this strategy widely for the last three or four years and have seen some decent success. This is typically used on popular items we sell all year, and is a way to offer some really nice savings for shopping holidays like Black Friday and Cyber Week. There are a lot of customers conditioned to expect these discounts and often wait for these sales events on products they know they need but have a relatively high price. You don't need to look farther than the ubiquitous Amazon and their Prime Days for an example of how deep discounts for a specific event can drive insane levels of purchases. In 2020, Amazon's Prime Day is estimated to have grossed more than $10 billion.[22]

Customer Loyalty Discount

---

22 Fareeha Ali, "Amazon's Prime Day 2021 sales total $11.19 billion," Digital Commerce 360, June 23, 2021, https://www.digitalcommerce360.com/article/amazon-prime-day-sales/.

We approach this method of rewarding loyal customers in two ways. The first method is to use a series of price tiers such as bronze, silver, and gold categories. As your purchases annually scale to certain levels, we move you into a new price category. Here's an example:

	Annual Purchases	Discount
Standard Price	0 - USD $50K	0%
Bronze Price	>USD $50K - USD $250K	5%
Silver Price	>USD $250K - USD $1M	8%
Gold Price	>USD $1M	10%

The second way of deploying a purchase discount is by way of a year-end rebate. Year-end rebates are deferred rebates granted by the seller at the end of each year (or according to any periodicity) to a key customer according to the fulfillment of their purchase commitments.   Normally these rebates are given as a credit notes issued by the sellers.

Crucially, year-end rebates control the pricing on the items throughout the year. If a customer promises to spend two-million dollars this year and wants gold pricing, but only ends up purchasing $500,000, you can't go back and raise the price. On the other hand, a year-end rebate rewards the customer for hitting a target.

Annual Purchases	Rebate on Annual Purchases
>USD $1M - USD $2M	1%
>USD $2M - USD $5M	2%
>USD $5M	3%

Shopping Cart Abandonment Discount

This discount method could warrant an entire book in itself, and keep in mind I'm not the expert in this area. The key takeaway is that roughly 70% of items in online shopping carts get abandoned, so it's of utmost importance to develop a strategy to recover them.[23] The key technique deployed is the automated abandoned cart email. To take things a step further, many companies are tempted to offer a discount for these carts. While I do suggest using the abandoned cart email, I don't recommend you automatically throw in a discount, particularly in technical sales fields, as it's not the best practice.

Sending an abandoned cart email helps customers who were distracted and forgot about the bill of materials they were searching for. Nudging them back to the cart is a helpful feature overall, but incentivizing them by providing a discount each time they log off can be habit forming and costly. If I was buying toilet paper from the same site and realized if I abandoned the cart briefly I could always get a discount, I would build this approach into my shopping strategy.

This is a double negative for my current supplier, because while I am logging off, I can easily be distracted by a competitor. Secondly, I'm driving down my own profits. The best time to deploy this strategy for me is during the initial purchase attempt. That can be a challenge, as it's usually the time when they have the "deepest pockets and shortest arms." Getting them to buy the first time can be tough, but once they're a customer it is completely different.

Bundle Discount

Product bundling is something I really love doing. In short, bundle pricing is a strategy in which a company or seller combines several products and then sells them at a single price instead of charging separate prices for each of them. The bundle is a product on its own since it has an ID, price, and attributes. This is a game changer for people googling your product code. Unique IDs will always send them straight back to your site. Combining various manufacturers items into one bundle also makes it difficult for other companies to match your solution.

---

23   "Reasons for Cart Abandonment – Why 68% of Users Abandon Their Cart (2021 data)," Baymard Institute, accessed Septmeber 13, 2021, https://baymard.com/blog/ecommerce-checkout-usability-report-and-benchmark.

Given the myriad of solutions we offer customers—from main units to cables to racks and cases as well as all the little pieces you need to connect and adapt things to one another— product bundling is a creative way to boost profits and performance on B brand accessories.   Customers are conditioned to perceive that they'll save more money by buying two or more items together rather than purchasing them individually. Typically, mixed bundling is offered, but it's important to note there's also the pure bundling methods as well. Here's how they both break down:

- **Pure bundling:** This is when the only way you can buy something is when it's bundled together with other products. More specifically, the products don't exist outside the bundle and/or can't be purchased that way. The easiest and most frustrating example of this is the dreaded cable TV bundle. How many times have you called asking for the NHL or NFL channel and your provider tells you, "Oh sorry, you have to get that with the sports bundle that includes a range of sports and outdoors-themed channels." They won't sell you individual channels. Further, pure bundling is broken down into either joint bundling or leader bundling.

  * *Joint bundling* is when the two products are offered together for one bundled price.

  * *Leader bundling* is when you combine a top selling product from leading brand with a discounted price if it's purchased with a non-leading brand product. For instance, you may have a large number of tool belts you are trying to sell and can include a top-name tool at a discount if they buy the tool belt.

- **Mixed bundling** is the practice of selling products both individually and in a bundle (which is usually priced below the sum of the individual product prices). The value meal (sandwich, fries, and soda) at McDonald's is a great example of mixed bundling.

Early/Prepayment Discounts

This is a popular discount we offer all the time to customers. If a customer is willing to pay up front and overlook net 30-day terms, which is more typical in our industry, we'll often offer them a one- to two-percent cash discount. We don't allow this if they're using a credit card, however, as the fees mitigate the savings.

Volume Discount

This refers to the use of discounted prices to incentivize a company to purchase a larger quantity at one time. If we can buy in bulk, we can pass on the savings we obtain directly to the customer. Typically, we expect the customer to take the full committed amount at one time. However, if they want it shipped over time, we blend the risk against the additional discount received and share a portion but not all the savings as our risk of being stuck with inventory goes up.

Free Shipping, DDP Destination

This tactic can be costly and the risks for DDP destination cannot be overlooked. DDP destination means the seller is responsible for all costs associated until the seller delivers the goods to the buyer, cleared for import at the named place of destination. In DDP, the seller does not pay for unloading the goods. Also, the risk of loss transfers at delivery, not shipping, so if the goods are lost in transit, it's on the seller to replace them. We try to ship FOB our dock, which means that the transfer occurs at the seller's shipping dock when the goods are safely on board the truck or ship. The buyer takes responsibility for the transport cost and liability during transportation. We can agree to pay for the shipping cost, but the risk is theirs once it leaves our dock.

Buy One, Get One Free (BOGOF)

Customers love getting free stuff. It's proven that customers typically overvalue in their mind the benefits of free, even when compared to higher-quality items at a discounted price. BOGOF is a proven sales tactic that creates a sense of urgency and can speed up customer purchase decisions.

Discount to Increase Factor

This is the *pièce de résistance* and namesake of this chapter, and it's a bit sketchy to be sure, but it's proven to drive behavior. Many of our manufacturers send periodic price increases that are firm. For instance, on June 1st, all prices are being raised four percent. The discount to increase factor happens when you raise the prices early and discount back to the current price during the transition period, as it is with the June 1st example of four percent. On May 1st, you raise all your prices by four percent and offer May Madness. Although it may seem a little sketchy or off base, it also has an additional hidden benefit. Everyone will see the new prices on May 1st, preventing people missing the deadline and expecting us to hold prices after June 1st when we can't. This gets more valuable as you get closer to May 31st.

CHAPTER 20

WITTSON PRICE FACTOR

I learned this back in the 1990s, and I have to say it was a genius strategy that I continue to deploy whenever I find myself not selling the number one brand. The first time I witnessed the Wittson Company was when I introduced a new tester, and they were the number two brand. They had a loyal base of customers but struggled with their 80% being the big guy's 20%. In other words, they usually only won 10% to 20% of the time.

The new tester was an all-singing, all-dancing, all-in-one beast with a color-touch screen, super-fast measurement times, and a promise of having fixed all the major complaints that had existed in prior models. At the time, the number one brand's main unit was selling for approximately $98,000 USD. With the incredible hardware we could offer, and what I was convinced was killer pricing, I thought that we would be unstoppable against the number one.

I was surprised the day marketing presented to the sales management team and we asked, "What's the street price?"

The marketing guy looked us square on and said, "One hundred and two thousand."

My jaw dropped. I couldn't understand why they were pricing the unit higher than the dominant market leader. It turns out I don't have an MBA in Marketing from Harvard or Yale, and I had a lot to learn.

When I questioned why we would do such a thing and not set the price at $89,000 or $93,000, the marketing manager quickly explained it to me. "Glenn, I understand your concern and we always grapple with pricing issues especially on major product launches. So, imagine this scenario. You're out showing the box to customers, and they fall in love with it. They have six units of the competition on the floor, and they say, 'So, how much?' and you respond proudly, 'Eighty-nine thousand, which is 10% less than you-know-who for 20% faster.' Some time goes by and you follow up and the guy says, 'Sorry, Glenn, we compared the measurements, and you are faster in some areas and not in others. You both handle all our measurements. We're comfortable with UI for the incumbent box and when they heard your new unit is selling for $89,000, they agreed to price match on all future sales, so we decided to stick with them.' They've done no work on this sale—all they had to do was discount and quote, and in the stroke of a pen, they wiped out our price advantage."

So then, the marketer said, "Now imagine you're asked the same thing and you reply, 'One hundred and two thousand, and we offer outright purchase and 12- or 36-month lease-to-own. Which would you prefer?' The customer is like, 'Oh wow, you're almost $5,000 more than number one.' At that point, the competitor can't do anything. If they discount their product to fight you off, they just sully their brand, as they're already cheaper. They can't raise the price, can they? No, you get to apply all your skills learned during GBL sessions and present the WSP in such a way that they're willing to pay more. If not, the compromise is you agree to price match if we lock this deal down this month."

The rule is when you're not the number one brand and don't enjoy the leader in market share position, you need to price your units just over the price of the leader. You'll learn quickly that pricing power is a skill. You need to learn the discipline, apply it daily, and teach everyone in your organization about it. Whether you have five, 50, 500, or 5,000 people, you need to choose to be the market maker and not an also-ran low-price hawker. The price chase is a fool's game. The bigger mistake is getting tricked into engaging in this game with your key customers where service, not price, is paramount. If you insist on discounting battles, you start to erode margin along with it, and that will erode your ability to service the account. The closer you get to zero-percent margin, the more you struggle to properly service the customer. You'll always default to deploying service levels on customers with reasonable profit levels. In other words, customers who are willing to pay for service!

For price models, there are three basic options to choose from. The one you choose defines the culture in your company and how your staff responds. There are times when you'll pick a single strategy, or you may adopt a blended strategy where you combine the most useful elements of each to your own unique values and the proposition you want to present. In my opinion, moving from cost-based pricing to rewarding value-based pricing is my goal.

The three strategies are:

- Cost-based pricing
- Competition-based pricing
- Value-based pricing

Here is a breakdown of how the model is derived:

1. **Cost-based pricing** is based on available cost parameters that are readily available from suppliers or accounting. These parameters include input cost, freight, duties, and local taxes. The company adds in either a target margin or a cost-plus percentage method or, if the product is strategic, they could use the math to derive a break-even price model. The downside to this strategy is what the customer is willing to pay isn't a consideration. Also, given the pricing is just straight math with a margin added on top, the competitor's pricing is not factored into the decision.

2. **Competition-based pricing** is pretty much exactly how it sounds, and in my experience, any time we've used this method, the results have been less than rewarding. My companies have chased the bottom dollar and ended up in bidding wars when the price can be the primary factor. Typically, one would base prices on competitive price levels or competitors' values for like rank products. It's similar to hearing the word "comps," meaning comparable, to real estate.

3. **Value-based pricing** is based on determining what the customer is willing to pay. From my experience, this approach is typically the most appropriate and most rewarding. If you can gain access to the high-volume plants for your products, the input cost is radically different than typical distribution chain pricing experienced from domestic supply lines. If you apply a cost-based approach and domestic margins, you'd destroy the market price for the items you are selling. For example, if you normally sell widgets for $39 to $49 based on size and shape and you normally make 25% to 35%, you then approach a high-volume offshore supplier and realize if you can step up to a production size lot, your cost will drop from $25 to perhaps five dollars. If you were so inclined to use cost-based pricing in this situation, you'd lower the market price to seven dollars. With all other North American suppliers selling this starting at $39, it's tantamount to insanity to offer something for seven dollars. Therefore, it is critical you determine the fair market price for the item while remembering some standard facts:

- Prices are derived based on how much customers are willing to pay.
- The value of the product is derived from the benefit it affords the customer.
- Like products from competitors can influence the value customers will perceive a product to have.

To achieve a realistic and useful value-based price, you'll need to take the steps required. If you're sourcing in high volume from Asia and paying two dollars a pack for something when you buy 10,000 units and the street price is $17.50 to $19.00, you need to understand your price is based on what your customers *are willing* to pay. In short, you need to know what that price is. This requires leg work and constant contact with customers who buy these products regularly to understand what they're currently spending. The answers you get will tell you the perceived value of products. You also need to branch out to newer customers wherever possible to figure out what these customers would be willing to pay for your products.

In a perfect world, all our competitors would use value-based pricing. However, with some items we run into outlier competitors such as import-export houses that treat your products like another piece of plastic or metal to buy in Asia and sell in North America. To that end, they typically compete on low costs and low prices. Value-based pricing offers key advantages. The price will typically fit with what the customer thinks the price should be and value-based pricing allows for much more profit per item when the research is done upfront. This is vital if you want to expand your offerings and grow your business.

Tenacious Takeaway Factor

Our last discount strategy is a hard one to pull off, but tough negotiators call for tough measures. Be prepared going into negotiations if you're going to deploy the tenacious takeaway. Suppose you're trying sell a product to Carl at AcmeTech and he's famously difficult on vendors, demanding huge concessions and resolute attitude not to purchase until he gets what he wants. In such a case you would be remiss to not go in fully prepared, knowing full well where the bottom line is on price. So, the street price for the unit you're selling is $11,400. Typically, you can offer up to a 10% discount, maintain margins, and be within vendor guidelines. But in this case, you have a deal registration and competitive discount in hand and are free to go 15% off.

The idea behind the tenacious takeaway works like this. You're talking to Carl and with some back and forth you move the price in a couple of steps to $10,260 (10% off). He's being his usual steadfast and belligerent self and saying he can do better. At this point, you or perhaps the manager feign discussion or communication and say, "Look, we can probably get a special dispensation to move this before month's end (this Friday) for $9,690 (15%)." At this point, Carl starts to perk up, as he realizes 15% is way more than usual. So, you now have to pull off the tenacious takeaway and again either leave and call him back or feign communication with HQ and explain. "Hey Carl, we messed up. We can't do 15% on that particular unit and need to recant the extra five percent."

Of course, Carl explodes, demanding compensation, special dispensation, and everything else under the sun and says, "Look, a deal's a deal! You said it, you honor it!"

"Ok, look, I'm probably gonna get fired over this, Carl, but if you can cut me an order now, I can claim it was too late and you'd already put it through. I'll leave it to the folks at HQ to discuss the bad news," you say.

"Ok, let's get this on the books, and they better not fire you or they'll have me to deal with," Carl says.

Obviously, this is a little sneaky, but when it comes to grinding the last dollar out of you, many customers will try every excuse and trick in the book. A little creative takeaway may be just what's needed to move a doggedly stubborn customer over the line.

Five by Five Breakdown Factor

Even though we sell some of the world's most advanced technologies, many of our customers look at our products as commodities. And given the myriad suppliers they deal with offering a vast array of technology items they need, they often feel your products are easily second sourced from other suppliers, and to that end, only price matters in the buying decision.

That's especially frustrating when you know the engineers did a careful evaluation and only your products meet the customer's technical needs.

The buyer should have *no other choice* but to suck it up and send you an order. But billion-dollar companies rarely approach your products this way. Instead, they break us down one piece at a time.

Everyone tries to drive efficiencies into their production—it means you can pass these gains to customers in the form of price reductions. But these price discounts often damage the equity in your brand, and there's no doubt everyone in the distribution suffers losses in profit margins. Once a customer is *rewarded* with a better price, they start to become disengaged and eventually reduce their expectations to a simple, "Here's the price I will pay." They aren't interested in your support, marketing communications, engineering enhancements, or anything else. It's all about the price.

Problem customers usually follow one, or many, of the examples below:

1. **Silent Sam**: These customers keep you in the dark and will withhold budget details and target pricing. They'll tell you the quantity and perhaps the timing, but they refuse to engage in price discussions, forcing you to make the first move. They assume that if they mention budget or price, it will miraculously be the exact number we will return with. Instead, they demand we lead with our best price.

2. **David Gleason**: A throwback to an earlier lesson, this customer will always counter your best price with the threat they can go elsewhere and have competitive quotes for the same or similar products from other suppliers.

3. **Freddie Free Shipping**: This customer never quits and will act incredulous about the cost and risk during shipping. This is a hidden killer that drives up costs, lowers margins, and most importantly can seriously change the risk profile based on DDP destination, FOB origin, and other terms that govern when the risk changes hands (i.e. our dock, their dock). Customers will always ask for our company to cover the shipping cost, and this is where you need to be resolute unless you're willing to take up to a five-percent hit.

4. **Willy Warton Warranties**: Here, the customer assumes extended warranties should be free. To the savvy buyer, they know this is a place they can inflict further margin reductions from a softer cost for the vendor. They love to ask for these items as well as upgrades, extra memory, and special packaging, and they suggest those are easy to throw in.

5. **Sorry Sally**: This customer gets the best possible prices but lets us know we lost the deal. She'll say, "Sorry Glenn, we love dealing with you, but I had three quotes and in fairness, you didn't come in with the best price. Feel free to let me know if there are any sales or promos that come along."

6. **Uncomfortable Unconstructor:** This person tears your deals down to its smallest possible pieces and works to dissect exactly how the vendor, the salesperson, and everyone within the chain makes their money. For instance, they'll beat up the sales guy until he reveals he gets paid little on the mainframe but top commissions on options and upgrades. He works to create a situation where he cajoles a lower price on the mainframe, only to pay full pop on the options.

7. **Delayful Darren**: He loves to string you along and delay deals as long as possible until you're at the end of a month, quarter, or year and are clamouring for deals to make your numbers. Smelling blood, they know you'll find every discount possible to make a deal before theses deadlines pass.

8. **Bad News Barry**: He has a keen eye on the news and industry insights. He's constantly searching for intelligence on your company and the industry for details like raw materials prices and exchange rates. He'll use any and every angle possible, and a usual focus is the improvement of the Canadian dollar to the U.S. dollar exchange rate. It could also be copper prices, lumber, or tariffs. This technique works especially well when an economic downturn is mentioned and they're threatening this could be the last deal for a while,

or that they'll have to reduce future order volumes in the absence of price concessions.

9. **Nicky Nicky Net 90**: This customer loves to beat us up on payment-term discounts. Our largest customers now have this built in. We can work with them and get paid net 60, but they offer portals we can access and take our payments anywhere from one to 59 days early. When we do, they get meaningful discounts. Smaller customers ask for prepaid discounts, two percent / net 10 day or cash discounts. If they can't wrangle discounts, they go the other way and ask for net 90- or net 120-day terms and want us to wait a third of the year to get paid.

10. **Intransigent Ingrid**: This is the toughest one we deal with, and is an example from the time I came up with the idea of five by five for a large customer we deal with. Typically, five by five means I hear you loud and clear. The saying for me came out as a play on words. One by one means they knocked us down in price. This customer started with one by one, then two by two, and three by three, and now we're at five by five. I think you get the idea. Essentially, Intransigent Ingrid applies everything noted above and then when it's all said and done and you've lowered the price to your bottom line, given 90-day terms, free shipping, and tacked on a three-year warranty, they go back to step one (Silent Sam) and stop communicating. They refuse to tell you what's wrong, no PO is issued, and finally when you get them on the call, they have a whole host of new demands. They're willing to wait months, or even a year, on a large purchase.

If you have the best product and have endured the base negotiations only to face one of these techniques, it's time to stand firm and be prepared to walk away. If it was always about the price, no one would drive a Mercedes Benz. You can drive a hard bargain, but at some point, you hit your final price and that's it. Remember one of our golden rules—freedom begins with no.

I Sold All the Demos

This is another good story from back in the late 1980s when I was a 20-something sales rep pounding the streets and learning all the factors I keep repeating here so often. You may remember the story about Albert Martin tearing the power cord from the wall during the demo for a customer who was acting rude and belligerent and passive aggressive about our presentation. This is not about that incident, but it is related to the item I was demo'ing that day.

As I mentioned in that story, we were selling EEPROM programmers, which are (to jog your memory, no pun intended) electrically erasable programmable read-only memory. It's a type of non-volatile memory used in computers, integrated in microcontrollers for smart cards and remote keyless systems, and other electronic devices to store relatively small amounts of data by allowing individual bytes to be erased and reprogrammed. The devices we sold allowed engineers and production workers to "program" these chips either one at time or in bulk by using a gang programmer.

Single Socket Programmer   **Gang Socket Programmer**   **FPGA Programmer**

 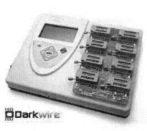 

The units above are similar to the ones I sold in the '80s. We'd accumulated numerous demos across the five offices my employer had in Canada, as these were popular since many of our customers used EEPROMs and FPGAs. One day the boss told us the company whose products we were selling was closing. They couldn't compete in this market, as the big guys had better resources to stay on top of all the programming issues that were required—especially as the market was evolving from EEPROMS to FP-GA's. They said, "Look, we have a ton of demos and we want to get rid of them before they close down." The summary table below shows quantities and SPIFs (salesman incentives) for selling each one.

	MSRP	Discount	Sale Price	Qty on Hand	Salesman SPIF
Single EEPROM Programmer	$ 2,499	50%	$ 1,250	6	$ 250
Gang EEPROM Programmer	$ 8,900	50%	$ 4,450	4	$ 1,000
FPGA EEPROM Programmer	$ 15,999	60%	$ 6,400	2	$ 5,000

So, given my young and greedy nature being honed to a fine art with the skills and greed-based learning, it took me no time to calculate there was $15,500 at stake in SPIFs. Even though it was before 9 a.m., I grabbed my briefcase with my callbook and with no time to spare, I started mentally compiling everyone that had ever bought a unit in the last four years.

I methodically set up my route, starting with area where the biggest ones were and mapped out a plan of attack. For most of the customers I skipped phone calls, only calling the few I needed to pre-alert my arrival. I set about to visit as many of those customers as I could get to. I went back to the office at three-thirty p.m. and headed straight into the boss's office. I burst in and proclaimed, "I sold all the demos."

He looked up at me and wondered what I was talking about. "What do you mean you sold all the demos?" he asked.

"Remember this morning, you printed off that SPIF sheet that listed all the programmers for sale?"

"Um, yes, those are good to sell, so go ahead."

"No Kim, you don't get it. I sold all the demos already. All those programmers you showed us this morning are sold. There's none left."

He was shocked, and thank goodness I had orders from customers, because the other salespeople were so busy at work they hadn't given it that much thought. They were pretty miffed though when at four p.m., the boss had to send out a memo saying, "Regarding those programmer demos and SPIF campaign we launched this morning. Well, I am happy to say in less than one working day Glenn sold all the demos and the promotion is closed."

When good deals come along, if you snooze, you lose. I made $15,500 extra that day plus all my normal commission and earnings. I can't begin to tell you how awesome that was.

Coffee is for Closers

I hope you enjoyed this book and will use it as a handy reference to avoid mistakes and gain useful tips for what you can do to further yourself in the eyes of the customer. I love to say that most of the time it's not about doing something right, but rather remembering all the wrong things not to do. For instance, we all know to say please and thank you, and it's just as important to remember not to talk with your mouth full.

One of the most powerful rules for me is to never sit in the lobby. It shows preparedness when the customer comes out to greet you, and it also shows the people you're with what the minimum standard of acceptable behavior is. Let's also not forget the rule to never forget a face, and that it's equally important to always have something in hand and something in your mind when you arrive to meet customers. I'm still going on calls today with my staff and I never miss an opportunity to ask for a mini-tour, as I'm always discovering things I could be proposing to the customer they're currently buying somewhere else. Finally, as we learned in WSP, by showing our Winning Sales Presence we are either increasing or decreasing our attractiveness in the eyes of the customer. Your job as a salesperson is to always take the next step towards increasing it and avoiding subjects, topics, actions, and behaviors that lower it. As we all know by now, attraction is not a choice! Thank you for reading.

Made in the USA
Coppell, TX
07 October 2023

22560748R00138